GHOSTS OF SLOCUM

by

Constance Hollie~Jawaid

&

E. R. Bills

2020

Ghosts of Slocum

Cover Design by E. R. Bills
Illustrations by Chais Adrian Teal

PREFACE

After author E. R. Bills and I won a hard-fought battle with the Anderson County Historical Commission (and others) for a historical marker to commemorate the 1910 Slocum Massacre, we decided to write a screenplay about the incident. We wrote the original version of what would become *Ghosts of Slocum* in 2016.

When E. R.'s book, *The 1910 Slocum Massacre: An Act of Genocide in East Texas* (2014) was optioned for film treatment in 2017, we mentioned our screenplay, but the first studio we encountered wanted it updated to the present day, making E. R. and I characters in a quest to get the Slocum Massacre story told. Our second run at a Slocum Massacre screenplay, *Shallow Playground*, was also strong, and it was optioned as well—but it now sits in limbo (check IMDB). So, we decided to release our original screenplay as a stand-alone manuscript.

The real story of the Slocum Massacre included some white protagonists, but they were bit players or promising postscripts. All of the antagonists were white and there was no white savior. The victims and heroes were all Black—boldly and powerfully Black. They represent the flesh and blood truth of my ancestors recorded in black ink. The black ink that tells the real story in the face of the negative white space on every page. And we've recorded their humanity and their Blackness in this narrative for everyone to experience. Unfortunately, there was no happy or satisfactory resolution to this story, and there probably never will be. So, we can't in good conscience provide a Hollywood ending.

Representatives and iconic parties from Hollywood, both black and white, have looked at this screenplay and don't know what to do with it. They say they like it, but I think they have some sense it can't be watered down—or that Mr. Bills and I will not water it down—so it gathers dust.

Until now.

We've published it here for you to experience the story yourself, in screenplay form. And I—the great, great, great granddaughter of Jack Hollie, one of the primary landowners in Slocum, Texas in 1910 and a high-profile target during the Slocum Massacre . . . I, a descendant of many who were murdered in cold blood during the carnage—ask that you consider this horrifying chapter in our history. You won't be alone. Just follow the black on the page.

Constance Hollie-Jawaid
July 29, 2020

ACKNOWLEDGMENTS

Without the continuous support and sacrifices made by my husband, Shereyar Jawaid, and by my children, Imani Ramirez and Edward Ramirez, I would not be able to do the work of seeking justice for the victims and descendants of the Slocum Massacre. I dedicate this work to several family members, including: my brother, my ride or die, Leo Hollie Jr., who is always there serving as an extra set of eyes and ears; my mom, Joyce Hollie, for her loving and nurturing spirit which encourages me to never give up the fight; three powerful men who taught me how to fight—my grandfather, Myrt Hollie; my father, Leo Hollie, Sr.; and my uncle L.D. Hollie. Their fight to seek justice for the victims of Slocum began many, many years before my birth. With their deaths, I vowed to continue their work. And finally, I dedicate this book to my great, great, great grandfather, Jack Hollie (Holley). He owned the only store in Slocum at the time of the massacre and many other businesses, including a dairy, granary and a co-owned all-Black bank. Papa Jack, thank you for passing along your business acumen and your indomitable seeds.

And, finally, I humbly dedicate this book to those who came before me—my Ancestors. Those Ancestors who incessantly whispered in my ear to "Remember Slocum". Those Ancestors who were killed during the Slocum Massacre.

With their guidance we will continue to fight for justice on their behalf.

Constance Hollie-Jawaid

FADE IN:

INT[1]—LATE-1970S SEDAN (SUMMER 1980)—DAY
FADE-IN to a little black girl, CONSTANCE, sitting next to the
driver's side door in the back seat. Her father, Leo Hollie, Sr., is
driving. Constance stares out the window taking in the piney
woods as they fly by.

>   LEO HOLLIE, SR.
>   (from the front seat)
>   All this, Constance . . . on both sides.
>   It was all ours. My granddaddy's.
>
>   CONSTANCE
>   Ours, Daddy? All ours?
>
>   LEO HOLLIE, SR.
>   Yes, ma'am, little girl. As far as you

---

[1] INT is a scene heading instruction that means interior. EXT means Exterior.

9

LEO HOLLIE, SR. (CONT'D)
can see. Every bit.

CONSTANCE
Can we stop and play? Can we go see
in the forest?

LEO HOLLIE, SR.
Not today, baby. But maybe someday.

FADE TO BLACK while Constance stares out the window.

—BUT WAY BACK in the black, there is a dim light. It grows
closer and larger and brighter. It's a campfire.

CUT TO:

EXT—PINEY WOODS—DARK NIGHT
Several black folks sit around a campfire in East Texas. There is
a small pile of logs next to the fire. In the background, the
low din of crickets is broken only by the occasional collapse and
crackle of burning logs in the campfire.

Prominent in the rough campfire circle are six men and two
women varying in age from 16-70. Some of the men and women
are field-hands or day-laborers. Their clothing evidences wounds;
the blood from the wounds has dried black.

Other black men, women and children move along the shadowy
periphery of the campfire, just outside the light. They, too, are
dressed in field clothes, and many are obviously wounded.

DICK, a gray-haired, black farmer in his mid-fifties, sits on a
large rock. Long strivings are etched in his features, and little
escapes his thoughtful gaze.

WILLA, a stout black woman in her mid-seventies, is seated on a
flat tree stump. She has thick gray hair and her soulful smile
conceals a fierce inner strength.

ALEX, a tall, black teenager sits on the ground near the campfire. He is handsome and jovial, the picture of effortless vitality.

JOHN, a bearded, ham-fisted, black man in his late twenties, is lying on his side facing the fire and using a knapsack for a pillow. There are as many dried blood splotches on his shirt as there are mends and patches in his trousers. The rest of the group are crouched, kneeling or sitting on the ground near the fire.

CUT TO:

EXT—PINEY WOODS—CONTINUOUS
Dick looks around the circle.

> DICK
> They comin.' Won't be long.

> ALEX
> How you know?

> DICK
> I know is all. I seen 'em.
> (rubs the back of his
> neck)
> I seen 'em 'round. And I seen white
> folks, too.

CLEVE, a nervous, black teenage boy with perpetually downcast eyes sits up suddenly.

> CLEVE
> (anxious)
> The white folks is back?

> DICK
> They ain't never left, Cleve. They
> never leave.

WILLA
This is foolish talk. Ain't nothing to it.
(turns to Dick)
Nothin' gonna change. White folks
don't talk about it. Why should we?

DICK
(with a nod
for emphasis)
Cause they don't.

Willa rolls her eyes.

CLEVE
(shaking his head)
I'm scared.

                    DICK
        We all scared, Cleveland. Everyone here
        is scared.

                    JOHN
                (dozing in and out)
        I'm tired.

The group is momentarily silent. RAE, a beautiful, black
teenage girl, who sits near Willa, grows perturbed.

                    RAE
        I don't wanna' talk about it anymore.

                    ALEX
        Me either.

                    DICK
        We gotta.

                    ALEX
        Why?

                    DICK
        Cause this may be the last time we
        together. We need to remember. No
        matter what happens, we got to
        remember.

The group is silent again.

Dick looks around at their faces, taking them in slowly. John's
eyes are closed.

Willa pokes at the fire with a stick. JEFF and SAM, on the
opposite side of the fire from Dick, are stoic. JEFF is a medium-
sized, teenage black boy; he is sitting on the ground.

SAM is a light-skinned teenage black boy who wears a tattered straw hat that has two large fish hooks single-stitched into the front brim. He sits next to Jeff.

Rae twirls a strand of her kinky hair with the index finger of her left hand. Cleve is unnerved.

>   DICK
>   (continuing)
>   Cleve?

CUT TO:

EXT—PINEY WOODS—CONTINUOUS
Cleve is sitting on the ground next to the fire. He doesn't answer.

>   DICK
>   (raising his voice)
>   Cleveland.

>   CLEVE
>   What?

>   DICK
>   One last time.

>   CLEVE
>   I don't wanna.

>   DICK
>   We got to.

>   CLEVE
>   Why I have'ta go first?

>   DICK
>   (patiently)
>   Cleve.

14

                    CLEVE
                  (frustrated)
         What! I done told it a hundred times!
         It don't matter. It don't do no good.

                                                CUT TO:

EXT—PINEY WOODS—CONTINUOUS
Dick is still seated on the rock.

                    DICK
                  (patiently)
         Cleve . . . tell it for us.
                  (nodding to the folks on
                       the periphery)
         Tell it for them.

                    CLEVE
         But why I gotta go first?

                    DICK
         Cleve. You know why. You wuz
         first.

                                                CUT TO:

EXT—PINEY WOODS—CONTINUOUS
Cleve shudders. Willa looks away.

Cleve starts to say something but nothing comes out. He looks at
Alex and then Dick. He shakes his head. A tear runs down his
cheek and he wipes it away.

                    CLEVE
         We spent the night at Aunt Ada's place.
         Me, Lusk and Big Willie. It wuz hot,
         but Aunt Ada opened the windows.
                  (eyes welling up)
         We got up early the next mornin' and

                      15

CLEVE (CONT'D)
Aunt Ada made us biscuits.
(wiping his eyes)
Wish I—dadgum, I wish I had me one
uh' them biscuits.

ALEX
They's the best.

SAM
You makin' me hungry, Cleve.

A faint smile flashes across Cleve's face.

CLEVE
We wuz walkin' to tend the cows and
horses. Milk'n, hay'n—whut we always
done.
(remembering)
Big Willie was runnin' his head and
Lusk wuz pokin' at him. Funnin' is all.
Nothin' mean.

SAM
Big Willie wouldn't hurt a doodle bug.

ALEX
(smiling)
Big Willie *is* a doodle bug.

WILLA
He always been a good boy.

Cleve leans up on his knees and then sits back on his heels.

CLEVE
Big Willie wuz carryin' on and then
we saw some white folks. We had
just crossed Ioni Creek and we seen

>   CLEVE (CONT'D)
> 'em in a clearing on the other side.
>   (pauses)
> I didn't pay 'em much mind till Big
> Willie stopped talkin.' I looked up
> and his jaw was slack, open, and
> he was starin' at them white men.
> I looked, too, and they guns was
> raised. Then. Then, they--*They shot
> me.*

Another tear rolls down Cleve's cheek.

                                        CUT TO:

EXT—PINEY WOODS—CONTINUOUS
The campfire group is listening intently.

>   SAM
> Did it hurt?

>   CLEVE
>   (another tear rolls
>   down his cheek)
> It knocked me down.

>   ALEX
> You said before it wuz like gittin'
> run over by a hog.

>   CLEVE
>   (sniffs)
> Yeah. Like a hog.

Cleve wipes his eyes and his nose with his shirt sleeve.

>   JEFF
> Is that when you seen Big Willie,
> when you seen Big Willie steppin'?

CUT TO:

EXT—PINEY WOODS—CONTINUOUS
Cleve smiles faintly.

> CLEVE
>
> Big Willie.
>> (pause)
>
> Yeah, Big Willie. I fell down and he
> and Lusk ran. Nothin' else they coulda'
> done. White folks started shootin' at
> us and wuddn't nothin' they could do
> but git shot, too. I fell down, but I seen
> Big Willie runnin'.
>> (starts to smile again)
>
> Big Willie do ever-thang slow, you
> know?

CUT TO:

EXT—PINEY WOODS—CONTINUOUS
Sam nods and rearranges his hat.

> SAM
>
> Slow as a mud turtle.

> JOHN
>> (mumbling)
>
> Slow as molasses.

Everyone looks at John, surprised. They assumed he was asleep.

> CLEVE
>
> It happened quick. White folks start'ta
> shootin' and I got shot, knocked me down.
> But I saw Big Willie runnin' like a train
> comin.' And he ketch Lusk.

> ALEX
>> (egging Cleve on)
>
> My little brother Lusk? No, sir. No how

19

CLEVE
(smiling)
Yessir. I'm tellin' it straight. Big Willie
passed Lusk goin' into the woods. He
ain't never stepped so quick in his life.

DISSOLVE TO:[2]

EXT—FAR SIDE OF IONI CREEK—MORNING
A solemn hodgepodge of white men (numbering around twenty)
—tall, short, some country and some city folk--raise their
shotguns, rifles and pistols and open fire on Cleve, LUSK and
BIG WILLIE.

SMASH CUT:[3]

EXT—NEAR SIDE OF IONI CREEK—MORNING
Cleve is felled immediately and Lusk, who resembles his older
brother, Alex (just younger and skinnier, and wearing some of
Alex's hand-me downs), breaks into a run. Big Willie, also a
teenager, but standing at least six-five under a flattened felt hat
(the front brim flipped up), and carrying every bit of three
hundred pounds, abruptly follows.

Big Willie removes his hat (after his first few steps) so he doesn't
lose it.

CUT TO:

EXT—FAR SIDE OF IONI CREEK—CONTINUOUS
The white men continue to fire on Lusk and Big Willie.

CUT TO:

EXT —AWAY FROM IONI CREEK - CONTINUOUS

---

[2] **DISSOLVE TO**: As one scene fades out, the next scene fades into place.
[3] **SMASH CUT**: One scene abruptly cuts to another for aesthetic, narrative, or
emotional purpose.

Lusk and Big Willie make it into a denser area in the woods and continue running. Bullets and buckshot splinter and pepper the trees and bushes around them.

Lusk runs straight into a low-hanging tree branch and it knocks him out cold. He collapses sideways and falls into a shallow ravine, rolling under a clump of thick briars. Big Willie passes nearby running through low-hanging branches.

CUT TO:

EXT—NEAR SIDE OF IONI CREEK—MOMENTS LATER
The group of white men walks past Cleve's prostrate form assuming he's dead. They head off in the direction that Lusk and Big Willie fled.

JUMP CUT:[4]

EXT—PINEY WOOD FOREST—MORNING
The group of white men walk past the ravine Lusk collapsed into, but never see him. They follow Big Willie's trail. It's a four-foot-wide swathe of broken limbs and small, flattened trees.

Big Willie is gone.

CUT TO:

EXT—PINEY WOODS—MORNING
Cleve finishes his story.

ALEX
Did you know any uh them white fellas?

CLEVE
(thinking)
Maybe one . . . by his talk.

---

[4] **JUMP CUT**: Transition conveying an abrupt time shift or passage, usually forward.

                    ALEX
          Was it Wirt?

                   CLEVE
          I don't know. Maybe

                   DICK
                (to Cleve)
          Did you find Lusk?

                   ALEX
          Lusk didn't say nothin' about it.

                                        CUT TO:

MEDIUM CLOSE—PINEY WOODS—CONTINUOUS
Cleve stares off.

                   CLEVE
          I didn't see him again. I don't know
          how long I wuz down, but when
          I got up I didn't see him. My head wuz
          heavy, I felt asleep at first. I walked for
          a long time and then . . . I wuz cold. It
          was real cold. But I saw a fire.

Cleve rubs his hands and holds them out closer to the campfire.

                                        CUT TO:

EXT—PINEY WOODS—CONTINUOUS
Alex leans in to warm his hands as well.

                   ALEX
          I didn't know who it wuz comin' up
          on me. It wuz getting dark that evenin'
          and I wuz tryin' to keep low. I
          heard someone comin'--I thought it
          wuz more white folks. I hid. Cleve

                      22

ALEX (CONT)
come limpin' up, all shot up, and I
saw him and came out.

CLEVE
I ain't never been so glad to see no one
in my life.

SAM
You wuz lucky. I got caught out by
myself.

Sam speaks out of turn and Dick stares at him sternly. Sam looks
at Cleve sheepishly and; Cleve looks at Sam and shrugs.

ALEX
Had me a poultice in my britches. After
I rubbed a patch of it up with some
leaves, I put some on Cleve's bullet holes
and some on mine.

WILLA
Where'd yah learn that?

ALEX
Uncle Abraham.

WILLA
Hah. I shoulda' knowed that. Abe runt
away when he was young and lived
with Wichita Indians for a spell. He
knew more remedies than me. Had a
poultice for anything that ailed ya'.

ALEX
Anythin' and everythin'. Couldn't walk
through the woods without him pointin'
at this and 'splainin' that. I thank I
remembered more than I thought.

                    DICK
That's a mouthful.

                    ALEX
Yeah.
                    (pause)
I surely miss him.

                    DICK
Me, too.

                    CLEVE
Me, too.

The group is lost in thought for a moment.

                    JOHN
                    (yawning)
        Me, four.

Some members of the group laugh. John never opens his eyes.

Cleve puts another log on the fire.

                    ALEX
My turn, I reckon.

                    DICK
Yep.

Alex stands up to stretch and then runs his tongue over his teeth.

                    ALEX
Well, a long time before Cleve come
up to my fire, 'fore lunch, I seen Lusk
and he wuz scared plumb outta' his
head. Had a big knot on his skull where
he say he run into a tree. Said tree
knocked him out. I say 'what you run

ALEX (CONT'D)
into a tree for?' He say 'cause white folks
done gone crazy.' He say they shot Cleve
and wuz shootin' at him and Big Willie.

CUT TO:

EXT—FRONT STOOP OF HOLLEY CABIN—DAY
Alex laughs. Lusk frowns.

LUSK
(gravely)
I ain't playin.

ALEX
White folks?

LUSK
I done toldja' they shot Cleve. An' they
May'uh shot Big Willie.

ALEX
Where?

LUSK
Right straight after we crossed Ioni
Creek. Down from Aunt Ada's.

ALEX
Show me.

LUSK
What if they still out there?

ALEX
We'll be careful. If yer sayin' the truth,
we can't leave Cleve out there. 'Sides,
we'll stay in the woods the whole way.

The boys stop at the Holley well and pull up a bucket of water. They share a ladle and drink.

                              ALEX
                          (continuing)
              Hold on.

Alex runs back up to the house and steps in momentarily. He steps back out and jogs over to Lusk. He has a poultice wrapped in a large leaf. He unrolls the leaf and sets it aside. He spits on the poultice, kneads it carefully and then rubs some on Lusk's knot. Lusk pulls away when Alex touches the knot.

                              ALEX
                          (continuing)
              Be still.

                              LUSK
              I stove my head in.

Lusk lets Alex rub a portion of the poultice across the knot.

                              ALEX
              You did not. I had worse places on
              my own eyeball. This'll help.

Alex wraps the remainder of the poultice back in the leaf and puts it in his pocket. Then the boys head out into the forest.

                                                    CUT TO:

EXT—PINEY WOODS—DAY
Alex and Lusk move through the woods quietly, keeping an eye out. Alex leads the way.

Alex and Lusk hear gunshots in the distance and get low.

                                                    CUT TO:

EXT—PINEY WOODS—MOMENTS LATER
Alex and Lusk stand again and start moving. They walk for
several moments and then Alex stops. There is a large blood-
splatter in the middle of the trail, and a body lies farther down.
Alex and Lusk step around the blood and approach the body.

The body is that of a young black man. He is lying on his
stomach, but his head is turned slightly sideways. He has been
shot in the back and is obviously gone.

                         ALEX
             You know him?

                         LUSK
             I seen him, but I don't remember
             his name . . .
                    (spotting another body
                         yards away)
             Uhhh . . .

                         ALEX
             What?

                         LUSK
                    (pointing)
             Over there.

                                              CUT TO:

POV⁵—PINEY WOODS—CONTINUOUS
Alex sees the body and they walk over to examine it. Another
black man lies dead, shot in the back.

Alex looks back at the first body. Both victims still have
knapsacks slung over their shoulder.

                                              CUT TO:

_____

⁵ **POV**-Point of View of character, in this case, Alex.

27

EXT—PINEY WOODS—CONTINUOUS

Alex shakes his head. Lusk stares at the far body.

> ALEX
>
> This the kinda' crazy you sayin' white
> folks is up to?

> LUSK
>
> Yes.

They hear more gunfire and the shots are closer. They both drop down.

> ALEX
>
> Sorry I didn't believe you.
> (pauses, thinking)
> Where's Mama and Daddy?

> LUSK
>
> I think they went up to Palestine in
> the wagon.

> ALEX
>
> We best make tracks thatta' way ourselves.
> I can't figure this. I don't understand what's
> happenin.'

Alex and Lusk hear a distant, blood-curdling scream and then three more shots--followed by laughter. Alex pulls Lusk close.

> ALEX
>
> (continuing)
> Let's git. We'll look for Cleve right
> fast and then go back to the house,
> see if anybody is there.

JUMP CUT:

EXT—PINEY WOODS —DAY
Alex and Lusk move quickly through the woods, utilizing cover
where they can. They find the swath Big Willie had cut through
in his escape and trace it back to the spot where Cleve was shot.

At the spot where Cleve fell, there is a significant pool of
blood—but Cleve is gone.

> LUSK
> He wuz right here.

> ALEX
> I can see that.
> (looking around)
> Let's get back to the house.

CUT TO:

EXT—PINEY WOODS—MOMENTS LATER
Alex and Lusk head back through the woods the way they came.
They hear intermittent gunfire in the distance.

Alex and Lusk come to a break in the forest and stop at the edge.

CUT TO:

POV—EAST TEXAS SKY THROUGH CLEARING—DAY
Alex and Lusk watch buzzards circling the sky in three separate
areas.

> ALEX
> See 'em?

> LUSK
> I see 'em.
> (gravely)
> This ain't good.

                         ALEX
           No, it's bad. It's done got real bad.

                                            CUT TO:

EXT—PINEY WOODS—MOMENTS LATER
Alex and Lusk dash across an open area and duck into another
patch of woods. They keep moving.

Alex and Lusk spot another body, that of an elderly black man,
face down and also shot in the back.

They don't stop.

                                            CUT TO:

EXT—FRONT STOOP OF HOLLEY RESIDENCE—DAY
Alex and Lusk run up to the house.

                         ALEX
                       (shouting)
               Mama?! Daddy?! Anybody here?

There is no answer, but their cousin, CHARLIE, a short teenage
black boy with a square jaw, a bushy unkept mop of hair and a
visible scar on his right cheek, crawls out from under the front
stoop.

                         LUSK
           Charlie!

                        CHARLIE
                       (mortified)
               What we done?! What we done?!

                         ALEX
           We ain't done nothin.

                           31

CHARLIE
Why white folks killin' us?

LUSK
We dunno. Anybody else come?

CHARLIE
No. Jus' me. I's walkin' through the
bottoms, mindin' my bizness. Started
hearin' shots and dirt wuz flyin' up around me.
I cut away, lickety-split. Made for some
woods and then snuck here.

ALEX
We thinkin' here ain't real safe neither.

CHARLIE
Where can we go?

LUSK
Palestine, we reckon. We think Mama
and Daddy are there.

CHARLIE
You seen my daddy?

LUSK
Uncle Abe, no.

ALEX
No. But we seen three bodies in the
woods comin' this way . . . and buzzards
all over. Uncle Abe won't git got less'n
he decides he wants got. Let's git.

CHARLIE
Okay.

The three boys head back into the woods at a jog.

CUT TO:

EXT—PINEY WOODS—MOMENTS LATER
They run for several moments, one after another in a loose line.
Charlie isn't wearing shoes and his feet are soon bloody.

> LUSK
> (to Charlie)
> Where yer shoes?

> CHARLIE
> I got scared. They come off when
> I's runnin'.

CUT TO:

EXT—SADLER CREEK—DAY
The boys slow down as they come to Sadler Creek. It's flowing
high and they pause to gauge where the best place to cross might
be.

As they investigate, they hear a whistle across the creek.

JUMP CUT:

EXT—FAR SIDE OF SADLER CREEK—CONTINUOUS
Sixteen white men (one on a horse) suddenly begin firing on
them.

JUMP CUT:

EXT—SADLER CREEK—CONTINUOUS
Alex and Charlie are felled immediately. Lusk is struck by a
bullet and spun around and dropped. As Lusk collapses,
Charlie begins to crawl away.

CUT TO:

EXT—PINEY WOODS—MOMENTS LATER

Charlie is hit in the left shoulder. He crawls on his right hand and knees for about ten yards and then gets up and runs.

CUT TO:

EXT—FAR SIDE OF SADLER CREEK—CONTINUOUS
The white men continue firing after Charlie.

JUMP CUT:

EXT—FOREST FLOOR NEAR SADLER CREEK—DAY
Alex and Lusk are lying very still right next to each other. Alex has gunshot wounds in his upper right torso and thigh and has bled profusely. Lusk has bled less but has wounds in the center of his abdomen and his left arm. The group of white men who'd just shot them is now passing by.

CUT TO:

EXT. FOREST NEAR SADLER CREEK - CONTINUOUS
Riding/walking point are WIRT, a grisly, white share-cropping miscreant in his early forties (on a horse) and MEEKS, a late twenty-something half-renter, sycophantic and fawning, especially toward Wirt.

>   MEEKS
> I don't think we'll be hearing any
> more outta' these niggers.

>   WIRT
> And you fellas was thinkin' there
> weren't no cure.

>   MEEKS
> Damn, Wirt.

>   WIRT
> Fixed 'em right up, didn't we?

34

Several men in the group laugh, but not DREW, a short, slight, bespectacled white man who is clearly growing uncomfortable with what they are up to. Behind him is MUNK, a young, gangly stable hand.

> DREW
> I knew these boys. They weren't no
> trouble.
> (under his breath)
> It's a damn shame.

> WIRT
> *Sheee-it*, Drew. Only shame is we
> only got two of the Holley boys and not
> their daddy, King Nigger Jack.
> (scoffs)
> My Elsie was in the Holley Mercantile
> the other day. She wuz short for some
> flour.

> MUNK
> Jack wouldn't give it to her?

Wirt stops his horse and turns to Munk.

> WIRT
> No—King Nigger Holley *did* give it to her.
> She got home and share tell of it with me,
> and I striped her thighs with a hickory switch.
> (spits)
> No self-pridin' son of the South needs help
> from a nigger.

CUT TO:

EXT—FOREST NEAR SADLER CREEK—CONTINUOUS
Wirt turns away from Munk and rides on.

WIRT

By the time Elsie kin sit down again,
She'll 'member that. And by the time
we finish 'round here, all the niggers'll
'member and keep to their station.

MEEKS
(overly enthusiastic)
Damn straight.
(pause)
Who let that nigger hang a shingle in
town in the first place? Word gits out
that Slocum has a darkie store and
folks'll be sayin' it's a nigger town.

Drew starts to say something but thinks better of it. The white
men move along and away.

JUMP CUT:

EXT—FOREST FLOOR NEAR SADLER CREEK—DAY
Alex's eyes are closed and he lies very still. Lusk opens his eyes
and slowly raises his head.

When Lusk is sure the white men are gone, he sits up and nudges
Alex. Alex is unresponsive.

LUSK
Alex?
(pause)
Alex!

Lusk nudges Alex again, but Alex is still unresponsive.
Lusk's eyes well up and tears begin streaming down his
cheeks.

Lusk sobs quietly.

> LUSK
> (continuing)
> *Alex.*

When his sobs subside, Lusk holds his wounded abdomen with both hands and slowly stands up. He looks around again to confirm that the white men are gone, and then he looks back down at Alex.

Lusk starts to kneel down to nudge Alex again, but the pain around the wound in his abdomen makes him stop.

Lusk gives Alex a light kick in the side, but Alex does not respond. Lusk says something to Alex under his breath and then starts to walk away.

CLOSE ON:[6] Alex's face. He lies very still.

MATCH CUT:[7]

EXT—PINEY WOODS—NIGHT
CLOSE ON: Alex's face. He is still standing in the middle of the campfire group, but his eyes are closed and a tear runs down his cheek.

> ALEX
> (opening his eyes)
> Lusk thought I was gone. I was hearing
> him, but I couldn't move.
> (wiping tears away)
> I woke up later, stiff and sore. And
> mighty parched.

CUT TO:

EXT—PINEY WOODS—CONTINUOUS

---

[6] **CLOSE ON**: A close-up on some object, action, or person or body part.
[7] **MATCH CUT**: Transition that cuts from one shot to another where the two shots are matched by the subject or action, in this case Alex's face.

The group around the fire is silent. Willa wipes tears away from her eyes as well.

                    ALEX
          I think Lusk made it and I'm glad'uh
          that. I wish I coulda' helped him.
                    (short pause)
          I took the poultice from my pocket
          and put it to my chest. I started makin'
          my way through the woods, but it started
          to git dark. That's when I built the fire.

                    CLEVE
          It was a sight for tuckered eyes.

A small black child from the shadowy periphery runs up to and then around the campfire. He smiles at Willa, and then disappears back out on the periphery.

Willa grins. Rae looks down and away.

                    DICK
               (regarding the boy)
          Looks like Jack's youngest, Marlon,
          dudn't it?

                    WILLA
          Same thaing runnin' through my mind.

                    DICK
          How ol' was he when . . .
               (thinking better of it)
          How old was he, Alex?

                    ALEX
          Not yet a year. Knee-high to a
          grasshopper . . . But crawlin' round
          like his britches on fire.

Dick looks at Rae and then John.

                    DICK
Is John awake?

                    CLEVE
Hard ta' say.

                    DICK
You with us, John?

                    JOHN
                (opening his eyes)
Huh?

                    DICK
John?

                    JOHN
Yeah.

                    DICK
It's your turn, John. You with us?

                    JOHN
Barely.

                                        CUT TO:

MEDIUM CLOSE—PINEY WOODS—CONTINUOUS
John tries to sit up, but the effort seems to exhaust him. He
slumps back. He closes his eyes again.

                    DICK
John.
                    JOHN
I'm comin', Dick. Jus' give me a
minute.

John's eyes open slowly. His eyelids flutter and blink.

                    39

                    JOHN
                 (continuing)
        It started . . .
                  (pause)
        I's at mah girl's house.

                                        CUT TO:

EXT—PINEY WOODS—CONTINUOUS
John stretches his arms and Jeff smiles.

                    JEFF
                  (kidding)
        Your lady friend's house?

                    JOHN
        No. Mah girl. Mah wife. I call her
        mah girl.
                  (pause)
        We ain't jus' been sweetheartin'. She
        been mah wife comin' up on a year.

John teeters, but his eyes stay open and he seems to focus.

                    JOHN
                 (continuing)
        I love her, mah girl. Name's Pearl,
        and that's whut she is.
                 (long pause)
        It started, I wuz at Pearl's house at that
        buggy-town 'tween Slocum and Percilla.

                    JEFF
        Buggy-Town?

                    JOHN
        Yeah.

                    JEFF
          What they call it that for?

                    DICK
          It's one a' tha' places white folks gather
          up day-help for the fields.

                    ALEX
          They call it a buggy-town cause white
          folks send a buggy wagon through there
          pickin' up and droppin' off. There's
          one up Alderbranch way, too.

John nods.

                    JOHN
          Mah girl had herself her own place
          there cause her and her first man
          built it they-selves 'fore he got sent
          to the prison farm for sassin' a field
          boss.
                    (short pause)
          When he got out, they 'cuse him uh
          killin' a white girl in Lone Star and . . .
          They burnt him. They burnt him
          alive.

                    WILLA
          They 'cused him uh killin' that Redden
          girl, but there wuddn't nuthin' to it. A
          white boy killed her and those devils
          blamed it on Lenny. That his name,
          John—*Lenny.*

                    JOHN
          Leonard. But they called him "Lenny."

                    DICK
          The Johnson boy. I remember.

                    41

ALEX

Me, too.

DICK

One of my cousins got a broke nose
Tryin' to stop the posse that grabbed
grabbed him.

John nods.

JOHN

I never knowed him, but I thank he
wuz a good fella.
(short pause)
Pearl is a good woman, but she had
her a rough time.

CUT TO:

MEDIUM CLOSE—PINEY WOODS—CONTINOUS
John closes his eyes for a moment and then reopens them.

JOHN

I ain't so much.
(pause)
None of you knowed me before. I wuz
no great shake. I wished no ill on her
man. I took things as I found 'em.
(sitting up)
I came round to help, but she wuz so
sad. And so pretty.
(long pause)
Pearl. That's what she is. A pearl.
Made me wanna be better than I
really wuz. Didn't never want her
to see I wuzn't near better than she
saw me. She gave me somethin' to
live up to, after I done run years livin'
down thangs.

43

JOHN (CONT'D)
(nodding his head)
I love her. She mah girl.

John raises up and looks around and out at the folks on the
periphery.

JOHN
(continuing, voice raised)
I love her. You see her, you tell her.

CUT TO:

EXT—PINEY WOODS—CONTINUOUS
The folks on the periphery hardly notice. The small group around
the campfire listens intently.

JOHN
(long pause)
It was mornin,' 'fore breakfast, first
shots I heared. They was *waaayyy*
off and away to the norwest. I didn't
worry none.

CUT TO:

INT—PEARL'S CABIN—MORNING
John and Pearl are sitting at a small table in the cabin, eating
breakfast. Pearl is several months pregnant--and striking. John
beams.

PEARL
Buggy gonna be here soon. You want
I could pack you some biscuits for
midday?

JOHN
No, girl—I got some jerky wrapped
up. You save 'em for you and her.

44

                          PEARL
              How you know it's a her?

John smiles.

                          PEARL
                       (continuing)
              I've a mind that that her's a he.

                          JOHN
              Heaven either way, Pearl. I be right
              proud. But I hope he's a she.

                          PEARL
              Why, John?

                          JOHN
                      (still smiling)
              I done tole you we got enougha' us
              Johns in the world—we short on Pearls.
              You and me, I reckon we could make a
              whole string of 'em an' they'd shine like
              they Mama.

                          PEARL
              You got it bad, Johnnie Hays, and
              I'm right sorry to disappoint ya'—but
              if she a boy I wuddn't gonna call him
              John.

                          JOHN
                        (laughs)
              Ha, well, like I said—we awwreddy
              got enough Johns in the world.

Gunfire sounds in the background. This time it is much closer.

                          PEARL
              What is it, John?

JOHN
I dunno. Buggy shoulda' been here
by now.

John gets up and goes to a side shutter and opens it slightly to
look out.

CUT TO:

POV—BUGGY-TOWN—MORNING
A red dirt road runs through Buggy-Town north to south, with
cabins spread along a half-mile stretch on both sides (Pearl's
cabin is on the south end).

John sees a small white mob carrying guns appear on the north
end of Buggy-Town.

CUT TO:

INT—PEARL'S CABIN—CONTINUOUS
John steps out onto Pearl's front stoop to get a better look.

CUT TO:

EXT—FRONT STOOP OF CABIN—CONTINUOUS
John comes out to have a look. His face changes immediately.

CUT TO:

POV—FRONT STOOP OF CABIN—CONTINUOUS
John watches the white mob begin shooting. They aim for the
black folks that are standing or walking out in the open.

CUT TO:

INT—PEARL'S CABIN—MORNING
John re-enters the cabin and steps back over to the side shutter.
He cracks it again and peers out.

                              PEARL
                   What's happenin', Johnnie?

                              JOHN
                   I dunno, sweetie.

John stares out the cracked shutter. His heart sinks.

                                               SMASH
                   CUT:

EXT—BUGGY-TOWN—MORNING
Black folks are fleeing their cabins and being shot down. Most
run into the surrounding woods and fields, but one young man
runs for his life down the red dirt road. John watches as a bullet
exits through the front of the young man's throat. The young man
falls face first, his hands at his sides.

As the number of open targets dwindle, the white assailants fire
into the cabins. When the bullets or buckshot strike the cabins,
they often elicit screams. If the members of the white mob hear
screams, they approach the cabin to finish the job.

                                               CUT TO:

INT—PEARL'S CABIN—MORNING
John shrinks back inside and secures the side shutter. His face is
suddenly ashen. He realizes they need to leave, but knows Pearl
will not be able to run, especially far.

                              PEARL
                   Johnnie?

                              JOHN
                   Grab some clothes and the biscuits
                   and throw them in a knapsack.

                              PEARL
                   What is—

                               47

                                JOHN
                          (interrupting)
                  Do it now, Pearl. Trouble comin'.
                             (pause)
                      We gots to hurry.

Pearl gathers a few clothes, wraps a couple of biscuits in a towel
and tucks them in a knapsack. John stands near the root cellar
door in the cabin floor.

                                PEARL
                John.

                                JOHN
                  No time. You gonna hear shootin',
                  Screamin,' mebbe even tauntin'.
                  Don't let it rile ya'.
                          (opens the small root
                            cellar door in the cabin
                                floor)
                Come here.

Pearl approaches and John takes her hand and kisses her gently.

                                JOHN
                          (continuing)
                  Get down in there and be quiet. Not
                  a whisper . . . no matter whatcha'
                  hear. Buggy-Town crawlin' with crazy
                  white folks. Trouble comin.'

                                PEARL
                What you gonna' do?

                                JOHN
                          (kisses Pearl again)
                  Ain't room fer both us in the root
                  cellar. I get you down there, I'm
                  gonna tear out the front and run into

                                  48

JOHN (CONT'D)
the woods . . . Draw 'em away. Hurry
up, now.

John helps Pearl into the small cellar. Pearl starts to cry.

JOHN
(continuing)
No call for that, girl. You my Pearl.
You my life. I be back.
(holding his index finger
to his mouth)
Shhhhhh.

CUT TO:

POV—ABOVE ROOT CELLAR—CONTINUOUS
John watches Pearl cover her mouth with her hand and smile at
him through her tears. He smiles back and slowly closes the
cellar door.

CUT TO:

INT—PEARL'S CABIN—CONTINUOUS
John suddenly shakes, but quickly regains his composure.

John pulls the table and a chair over to the cellar door to conceal
it. He grabs his jerky bag and cracks the front door. The mob is
close.

CUT TO:

EXT—PEARL'S CABIN—MORNING
John steps out the front door and runs south.

BUGGY-TOWN ASSAILANT #1
(spotting John)
Nigger!

BUGGY-TOWN ASSAILANT #2
Get 'im.

CUT TO:

EXT—SOUTH SIDE OF BUGGY-TOWN—MORNING
Two Buggy-Town assailants run after John. One stops to shoot.

John breaks east into an open field.

Both white men chase John now, and another joins in the pursuit.
The last pursuer cuts through Pearl's yard to join the chase. Pearl
never makes a sound.

CUT TO:

EXT—FIELD SOUTH OF BUGGY-TOWN—MORNING
John runs across the field. A bullet flies past him and he drops his
jerky sack and accelerates to a full sprint.

The white men get winded. They all stop running and start
shooting.

CUT TO:

INT—ROOT CELLAR UNDER HOUSE—MORNING
Pearl's hand is still over her mouth. She hears shots and neighbors
screaming but remains still and silent.

CUT TO:

EXT—BUGGY-TOWN—MORNING
A dozen black bodies lie in yards, on cabin stoops and along the
red dirt road. A young woman and her small son lay unconscious
and deathly still around the side of one cabin.

JUMP CUT:

EXT—PINEY WOODS—AFTERNOON

John is resting behind a patch of trees. He hears voices. John hugs one of the trees and eases up slowly. He sees white men approaching from the direction he was heading. One is on a white horse.

John eases back down and starts to crawl in the direction he came from. After he feels he's out of range he stands up and starts running.

The white men that had been approaching from the opposite direction spot John and begin shooting. The first several shots miss, but one bullet catches John in the upper back and exits under his right clavicle. John grunts and falls, but rolls forward and keeps running.

John tucks his right arm in and keeps running. He smiles and laughs; he can still run.

> JOHN
> I'm comin,' Pearl. I'm comin' girl.

> JUMP CUT:

EXT—PINEY WOODS—LATE AFTERNOON
Buggy-Town Assailant #2 and the third pursuer have abandoned the hunt and turned back. Buggy-Town Assailant #1 is sitting on the ground next to a large pine tree.

Buggy-Town Assailant #1 hears someone approaching and his resolve is rekindled. He slowly gets up on his knees and sees John.

> CUT TO:

POV—PINEY WOODS—CONTINUOUS
Buggy-Town Assailant #1 lets John get within twenty feet and then stands up and shoots. The gunshot knocks John backwards.

> CUT TO:

EXT—PINEY WOODS—CONTINUOUS
John falls, surprised, and lands on his back on the forest floor.

CUT TO:

INT—ROOT CELLAR—LATE AFTERNOON
Pearl is still sitting silently in the root cellar. Her eyes well up as she holds her pregnant belly with both hands.

CUT TO:

EXT—PINEY WOODS—LATE AFTERNOON
CLOSE ON: John's face. He stares at the sky through the forest canopy.

MATCH CUT:

EXT—PINEY WOODS—NIGHT
CLOSE ON: John's face. He stares at the campfire in silence. He seems to be seeing something, mulling something over. He is stuck. Everyone watches him, rapt in their attention to his account.

> DICK
> (trying to break the
> spell)
John?

CUT TO:
MEDIUM CLOSE—PINEY WOODS—CONTINUOUS
John sits silently for a moment.

> JOHN
> That's all I remember. Til I got here.

> ALEX
> Did you see Pearl again?

                              JOHN
        Not yet.
                         (leaning back)
        Not yet.

                                                      CUT TO:

EXT—PINEY WOODS—CONTINUOUS
John settles back on the ground. The small group around the
campfire watches him.

                              DICK
                 Awful brave, John.

                              JOHN
            I don't know. I don't reckon it that way.
            To my mind, I ain't never been brave
            a day in mah life. But I love me a fine
            woman . . . and she love me. *Me*.
                         (pause)
            That stands me up more than courage.
            I reckon it makes me plumb scary.

                             ALEX
                          (joking)
                 When you awake.

Cleve, Sam, Jeff and Willa laugh.

                             JOHN
                      (smiles weakly)
               When I'm awake—yeah.
                   (closing his eyes again)
            You know what I'm gonna do when I
            get back to Pearl's?

                             ALEX
        What's that?

                              53

                    JEFF
                (ribbing John)
        Take a nap?

More laughs. John smiles, opens his eyes and looks at Alex.

                    JOHN
        Make Pearl and me a bigger root cellar.

Laughs all around.

John continues to grin and closes his eyes again. Cleve gets up, places two logs on the fire and sits back down.

Dick stares at the fire and then looks up at the sky. Alex's eyes follow Dick's.

                    DICK
            Pretty out, idn'it?

                    ALEX
            Yup. That's Casso-peia.

                    DICK
        Casso-what?

                    ALEX
                (pointing)
        Casso-peia.
                    CLEVE
                (looking up)
        Where?

                    JEFF
                (looking up)
        Where?

                                    CUT TO:

EXT—NIGHT SKY—CONTINUOUS
In the vicinity of the Cassiopeia Constellation.

                    ALEX
          Over there.
                    (short pause)
          You see that "M" there?

                    WILLA
          I don't know my letters.

                    DICK
          I think I see it.

                    ALEX
          It's close to the North Star there. See
          it?

                    JEFF
          The Drinking Gourd?

                                        CUT TO:

EXT—PINEY WOODS—CONTINUOUS
Excepting John, the campfire group are all looking up.

                    ALEX
          Yep. The North Star is the end of the
          Drinking Gourd. White folks call it
          the Little Dipper. Casso-peia dances
          'round close to it.

People on the periphery of the campfire start to look up, too.

                    CLEVE
          I see it.

                    ALEX
          That's Casso-Peia. Right now it's

ALEX (CONT'D)
an "M" leanin' right.

WILLA
I wish I'duh learnt my letters.

ALEX
It's leanin' now, so I reckon it's
around four o'clock in the mornin'.

Alex turns to Willa and draws an "M" in the air with his finger.

ALEX
(continuing, to Willa)
Like two mountains.

CUT TO:

MEDIUM CLOSE—PINEY WOODS—CONTINUOUS
Willa and Alex are standing together looking up.

ALEX
(pointing)
When it turns into a straight "M," it'll be
right at six o'clock, dawn—we'll won't see it.
This evenin' at six o'clock it'll flip and be a
"dubya" Then at midnight, it'll be a "three."

WILLA
I know my numbers.

ALEX
We'll see that "three" at midnight.

CUT TO:

EXT—PINEY WOODS—CONTINUOUS
John turns and mumbles.

                    JOHN
Queen . . .

                    ALEX
What, John?

                    JOHN
African . . . Queen.

                    SAM
What?

                    ALEX
Yep.

                    DICK
What'd he say?

                    ALEX
Casso-peia. She was a Queen of Ethiopia.
In Africa.

                    CLEVE
Yeah?

                    RAE
A queen?

                    ALEX
Yeah. Way back. But now she suppose to be
chained to a chair up there. So she just move
round and round.

                    RAE
Whut for?

                    ALEX
Cause she thought she wuz pretty. They
punished her because she thought she

                    57

ALEX (CONT'D)
wuz pretty.

Short silence.

RAE
She is pretty.

DICK
She sure is.

Excepting John, the group stares at Cassiopeia. Her fate strikes an unexpectedly heavy chord in their breasts and they're quiet again.

RAE
(to Alex)
Who learnt you that?

ALEX
My daddy—Papa Jack.

WILLA
He always knowed a heap uh thangs.

DICK
Yeah, he does.

ALEX
He said he learnt it when he was young. Said most slaves tracked the North Star with the Drinking Gourd. But that Casso-peia was 'tween the two and she always helped him figure out where the North Star was.

The stargazers eventually go back to their spots around the campfire.

Rae lingers, but finally takes her spot as well.

> DICK
> Sam.

> SAM
> Yessir.

> DICK
> You ready to tell yours?

> SAM
> (looking at Dick)
> I reckon so, sir.

Sam continues looking at Dick, as if waiting for a signal.

> DICK
> Well, go on, son . . . 'fore the
> roosters crow.

> SAM
> Oh. Okay. Well, I reckon I'm a
> mite embarrassed.

> DICK
> Don't be.

CUT TO:

EXT—PINEY WOODS—CONTINUOUS
Sam nods.

> SAM
> I heard the shootin', it was all over,
> loud and ever-where. But I wuddn't
> sure what wuz goin' on.

CUT TO:

EXT—EDGE OF HARVESTED COTTON FIELD—NOON
Sam is walking to town. He pulls his hat down to keep the sun
out of his eyes. His path takes him into the woods.

CUT TO:

EXT—PINEY WOODS—MOMENTS LATER
Sam hears some shots and looks in their general direction. He
keeps walking and eventually sees a group of white men.

CUT TO:

EXT—SMALL CLEARING—CONTINUOUS
NOBLE, a large white man wearing faded long-johns under
trousers held up by well-worn leather suspenders, stands out
among the white men.

Alongside him is LANHAM, also large, a little older and more
neatly dressed.

NOBLE
(shouting)
Say, nigger!

SAM
Yes, Mr. Noble?

NOBLE
Come over here, boy.

Sam complies. He walks to the edge of the group of white men.
They all turn and face him.

Sam notices for the first time that they all have guns.

NOBLE
(continuing)
You seen your Uncle Gus, boy?

                    SAM
                (looking down)
        No, sir.

                    NOBLE
        Wouldja' tell us if you had?

                    SAM
                (looking down)
        Whatchoo' mean sir?

                    NOBLE
        I mean have you seen Deaf and Dumb
        Gus?

                    SAM
                (looking down)
        No, sir. But I can get him for ya'.
        Whatchoo' need him for?

                    NOBLE
        We got somethin' for him.

                    SAM
                (averting his eyes)
        Want that I should run it to him?

                    NOBLE
        No, boy. We have to give this to
        him eyeball to eyeball.

Noble cracks his double-barrel shotgun open and replaces both of
the shells.

                    LANHAM
                (intervening)
        How fast can you run, Sam?

SAM
I don't know, sir.

Noble glares at Lanham, but Lanham ignores him.

LANHAM
I betcha' can really pick 'em up and
put 'em down.

Sam doesn't know what to say.

LANHAM
(continuing)
You been a good boy, Sam.
(looking sternly at Noble)
So we're gonna give you a chance.

Noble is irritated, but he doesn't interrupt.

SAM
Whatchoo' mean, sir? You want I should
fetch Gus?

NOBLE
Nahhhh, Sam. See . . . we been on a
nigger hunt since this mornin'. I 'bout
got my limit, but the rest uh these boy
they still a lil' shy.

As Sam processes what Noble is saying, he raises his head, his
whole body tensed. He notices for the first time that most of the
white men have their guns trained on him. Sam steps back, as if
about to break for a run, but he knows it is no use. Three of the
men have him in point-blank range.

NOBLE
(lowering his rifle, continuing)
I got me a haff-dozen niggers, at least.

NOBLE (CONT'D)
If ya' count nigger babies, mebbe a few
more.

Sam starts to say something, but holds his tongue.

NOBLE
(continuing)
Most of 'em wuz runnin' 'way—even
the nigger babies.
(smiles at Meeks and Munk)
You tha' first nigger that done walk
right upta' us, pretty as ya' please.

Sam is terrified, but also enraged.

NOBLE
(continuing)
Ya' got sumpin' to say, Sambo?

LANHAM
(glaring at Noble)
Shut-up, Noble.

CUT TO:

MEDIUM CLOSE—SMALL CLEARING—CONTINUOUS
Lanham turns to Sam and smiles.

LANHAM
I ain't never forgot how you minded
them trout-lines for me when you was
a boy, Sam. We got no kick with you.
(short pause)
But today is not y'all's day—

CUT TO:

MEDIUM CLOSE—SMALL CLEARING—CONTINUOUS

Noble interrupts Lanham and glares at Sam.

> NOBLE
> You darkies been niggerin' up thangs
> around these parts since the war ended
> and we decided we done had enough.
> Slobberin' over our women. Prancin'
> 'round after that Johnson nigger waylaid
> Jeffries. Thankin' you *done* sumthin.
> Thankin' you *is* sumthin. You been
> Disbehavin' in general. And we aim to
> fix it.

Sam trembles. Noble snickers.

> LANHAM
> You know yer numbers, Sam?

> SAM
> Yessir, most of 'em, sir.

> LANHAM
> We gonna give you the count of
> twenty 'fore we come for ya.

Lanham nods at Noble. Noble gives him a look and then points his shotgun in the air.

> LANHAM
> (continuing)
> Go on, Sam.

Noble fires his gun into the air.

Sam sprints away in the direction he came from. He forgets to count.

> NOBLE
> *Woooeee.* Look at that nigger go!

CUT TO:

EXT—PINEY WOODS—AFTERNOON
Sam is gliding through the woods, his straw hat in his right hand. He ducks and dodges limbs.

Sam hears shots in the distance and slows. He looks around and realizes he is close to Ioni Creek.

CUT TO:

EXT—WOODS NEAR IONI CREEK—AFTERNOON
Sam jogs down to the creek's edge. The creek is at its thickest point there, and he does not feel comfortable crossing it.

Afraid Noble and the others are close behind, and more may lie ahead, Sam is also hesitant to return to the path. A giant oak tree stands next to Ioni Creek and Sam has an idea.

CUT TO:

EXT—PINEY WOODS—AFTERNOON
The group of white men are a bit behind Sam but moving steady. Noble is in front with Lanham.

Noble laughs and shakes his head. Lanham ignores him.

NOBLE
(with a sideways glance)
Awful soft on 'im, huh, Lan?

LANHAM
You tryin' to' say somethin', Noble?

NOBLE
I said it. I said you wuz soft on 'im.

LANHAM
I heard'ja.

NOBLE
(laughs)
He is, then.

LANHAM
Is what?

Noble stops. The rest of the group stops as well. Noble grins at
Lanham.

NOBLE
He's one a' yers, ain't he?

Lanham turns and jams the butt of the rifle he's carrying into
Noble's gut with both hands. Noble collapses like a sack of
potatoes and lays on the ground, gasping for breath.

LANHAM
(standing over Noble)
I recommend you mind yer tongue,
Nobless Meacham. Before I pull it out
and wrap it around yer neck.

Noble coughs and sputters, slowly regaining his breath.

LANHAM
(continuing)
We got uh chore to do, an' I'm doin' it. But
I don't take kindly to reckless talk.

Noble starts to breathe again.

Lanham straightens up, looks around and then leans back over
Noble.

LANHAM
(holding out his hand
to help Noble up)
We straight?

Noble looks up at Lanham and hesitates. They stare at each other hard.

Noble extends his hand and Lanham pulls him up.

CUT TO:

EXT—GIANT OAK TREE—AFTERNOON
Sam is climbing the tree. He hangs his straw hat on a low limb and notices the white shirt he's wearing comprises a stark contrast to the green leaves, the brown tree bark and his brown skin. He pulls the shirt off and tucks it into his britches.

Sam climbs until he reaches a thick branch approximately twenty feet up. He straddles another branch on the side of the tree facing Ioni Creek and rests.

CUT TO:

EXT—PINEY WOODS—NIGHT
The campfire group is listening in their spots around the fire. Alex finally sits back down.

SAM
I saw somethin' after . . . *surprise me.*
Surprise me so much I dang near fell
outta tha' tree.

ALEX
Tell it.

SAM
Didn't know what it wuz at first. The
Ioni was up and it came floatin' down.
Thought it wuz a big ol' clump-uh ants
at first. Or dirt. But it wuzn't fallin' apart.
And it seem wallered out?!

CUT TO:

EXT—GIANT OAK TREE—AFTERNOON
Sam is in the giant oak tree looking down. A wooden barrel is floating down the creek. Sam leans and squints.

CUT TO:

POV—IONI CREEK—AFTERNOON
Sam watches as the barrel floats down the creek.

As the barrel approaches the giant oak tree, an elderly black man's gray head rise up from the barrel, and he looks around.

CUT TO:

EXT—GIANT OAK TREE—AFTERNOON
When Sam sees the old man look up out of the barrel, he almost exclaims out loud. He smiles and moves in the tree.

CUT TO:

POV—IONI CREEK—CONTINUOUS

Sam watches the old man in the barrel pass under his perch in the tree. The old man sees Sam and a little girl stands up in the old man's lap.

The old man smiles at Sam and waves. The little girl sits back down in the barrel and the barrel floats downstream.

CUT TO:

EXT—GIANT OAK TREE—CONTINUOUS
Sam watches the barrel until its gone. Then, he turns in the tree and surveys the path he came from (before he turned toward the creek).

He is wary of the men that are coming for him.

CUT TO:

POV—GIANT OAK TREE—CONTINUOUS
After a few moments, Sam sees Noble appear with the rest of the men in the group behind him. Lanham now takes up the rear.

CUT TO:

EXT—GIANT OAK TREE—CONTINUOUS
Sam stealthily slips around the tree to the side opposite of his pursuers.

CUT TO:

EXT—PATH—CONTINUOUS
Noble and the group approach, still on the path Sam turned off of.

> WHITE SEARCHER #1
> That coon lit out, didn't he? He's
> probably to Little Rock by now.

> WHITE SEARCHER #2
> He run like a deer. We ain't
> likely to ketch him.

> WHITE SEARCHER #1
> Mebbe we shoulda' brung our horses.

> NOBLE
> (now surly)
> Jus' keep yer eyes peeled.

> WHITE SEARCHER #1
> Wonder how the other fellas is doin'?

> WHITE SEARCHER #2
> They had 'em a passel 'fore lunch.
> Lurchmon has his daddy's ol'
> Spencer Repeater.

71

NOBLE
Still plenty uh daylight left.

CUT TO:

EXT—GIANT OAK TREE—CONTINUOUS
Sam hardly breathes. He remains motionless until the group passes.

CUT TO:

EXT—EAST TEXAS FOREST—LATER
Sam is back on the ground and has his shirt on. He steps back toward his original path and begins to retrace his steps. He hears someone behind him and freezes.

LANHAM
Turn around, Sam.

Sam slowly turns around. Lanham is standing alone.

LANHAM
(continuing)
I told you to run, boy. Why'd ya stop?

SAM
I reckon I was foolish, Mr. Lanham.

LANHAM
I wasn't sure you'd hung back, but I reckoned it was possible. Wasn't even really tryin' to find ya.'

SAM
(nodding toward a tree)
I was tryin' to hide in that big oak yonder.

                    LANHAM
                 (looking over)
          Look at that old giant. Reckon he's
          seen it all.
                    (pause)
          You wuz always smart.

Lanham lowers his gun. He stares at it momentarily, and Sam
contemplates running.

                    LANHAM
                 (continuing)
          Why you reckon God made some folks
          white and some folks black, Sam?

                    SAM
          I don't know, Mr. Lanham.

                    LANHAM
          I can't get mah head 'round it. The
          question is too big, but I don't see no way
          it makes sense.

                    SAM
          My Mama say God made man from the
          dirt of the earth and we the same color
          of the earth. She say—

Sam holds his tongue.

                    LANHAM
          Go ahead, Sam.

                    SAM
          My Mama say we the color of earth
          and white folks the color of sand in an
          hourglass.

Lanham smiles.

LANHAM
Some truth to that, I reckon. How is
your Mama?

SAM
She alright. She cannin' today.

Lanham looks at Sam and then looks away.

LANHAM
She was somethin' when she was your
age.
(smiles, thinking)
So was your Daddy.

SAM
You knowed my Daddy, Mr. Lanham?

CUT TO:

MEDIUM CLOSE—PINEY WOODS—CONTINUOUS
Lanham smiles wistfully and glances at Sam.

LANHAM
I did, Sam. I knew your Daddy.
(looking away again)
I used to know him.

Lanham is pained by a memory, and clearly troubled by the
circumstances in general. Lanham stands silent for a moment and
then returns his attention to Sam.

CUT TO:

EXT—PATH—CONTINUOUS
Sam is tense and afraid. Lanham begins to approach Sam with his
gun at his side. Lanham hopes Sam will make a break for it, but
Sam has already considered his odds.

LANHAM
I hate all this, Sam . . .

Instead of running away, Sam suddenly lunges for Lanham's
rifle and catches him off guard.

Lanham accidentally shoots Sam in the side, but Sam grabs hold
of the barrel of the gun and tries to wrest it from Lanham's grip.
They struggle momentarily and the rifle fires again, striking Sam
for the second time.

LANHAM
(continuing)
Sam!

Sam grunts and stumbles backwards. Lanham falls down and
drops his rifle. Sam turns and begins to flee.

CUT TO:

MEDIUM CLOSE—PATH—CONTINUOUS
Lanham is sitting on the ground, stunned.

LANHAM
Sam. *Sam!*
(mumbling)
I didn't mean . . .
(shouting after Sam)
Sam!

CUT TO:

EXT—PATH—MOMENTS LATER
Noble and the rest of the men return at a jog.

CUT TO:

EXT—EAST TEXAS FOREST BRUSH—CONTINUOUS
Sam ducks in some brush not far away and eases himself down

to the ground. He holds his side and lies on his stomach.

CUT TO:

POV—PATH—CONTINUOUS
Sam can see Lanham. As Noble and the others walk up, Lanham is staring at his own hands.

> WHITE SEARCHER #1
> You awwight, Lanham? *Didja' git him?*

> LANHAM
> (visibly shaken)
> I . . . I. Yes.
> (distraught)
> Yeah, I got him.

CUT TO:

EXT—PINEY WOODS—AFTERNOON
Noble and the White Searchers are standing around and near Lanham.

> WHITE SEARCHER #1
> (helping Lanham up)
> You drop yer rifle?

> LANHAM
> (staring in the direction
> Sam ran in)
> Yeah.

White Searcher #1 picks up Lanham's rifle and hands it to him.

> WHITE SEARCHER #2
> You want us to go fetch 'im?

> LANHAM
> No!

LANHAM
(short pause)
No. Leave him be. He won't get far.

NOBLE
We'll go finish him off.

LANHAM
(shaky, but angry)
I said no.

Noble turns to face Lanham. They glare at each other.

Noble averts his glance.

LANHAM
(continuing)
No. *Please.*

Noble and the White Searchers look at one another and then at Lanham.

CUT TO:

MEDIUM CLOSE—PATH—CONTINUOUS
Lanham's features change and seem to sink. Something is visibly wrong. He stares off at nothing. He takes a long breath and trembles.

CUT TO:

EXT—PATH—CONTINUOUS
Noble and the others are surprised. They watch Lanham in something like astonishment.

NOBLE
Lanham.

CUT TO:

MEDIUM CLOSE—PATH—CONTINUOUS
Lanham doesn't respond. His eyes well up and his bottom lip begins to quiver.

> NOBLE
> Lanham?

CUT TO:

EXT—PATH—CONTINUOUS
Lanham suddenly places the barrel of the rifle in his mouth.

> NOBLE
> (continuing)
> *Lanham!*

Lanham pulls the trigger and blasts a large chunk of the back of his head off. He takes one half-step backwards, teeters and then crumples to the earth.

CUT TO:

EXT—PINEY WOODS BRUSH—AFTERNOON
Sam sees it all. The back of Sam's free hand (balled into a fist) covers his mouth. Sam's eyes are wild and scared.

Sam stares for a long moment and then stops and gingerly rolls over on his back. He wipes his eyes with the back of the same fist and then lies still and listens.

CUT TO:

EXT—EAST TEXAS FOREST—AFTERNOON
CLOSE ON: Lanham's dying eyes stare at the dirt. They blink and flutter.

CUT TO:

EXT—PATH—CONTINUOUS

White Searcher #1 regurgitates. Noble and the others look on in shock.

                    WHITE SEARCHER #2
          I ain't never seen the like . . .

Noble stares in disbelief.

The last tremors of life in Lanham are quickly extinguished.

                    WHITE SEARCHER #1
                    (wiping his mouth)
          You want us to go find the nigger?

Noble does not respond.

                    WHITE SEARCHER #1
                    (continuing)
          Noble?

                    NOBLE
                    (long pause)
          No. Let's get on down the trail.
                    (short pause)
          We'll send somebody back with a
          wagon for Lanham.

The white men move on.

After several moments, Sam limps up cautiously.

Sam looks in the direction that Noble and the White Searchers headed off in to make sure they are gone.

Sam stares at Lanham's motionless body for a moment and then turns and limps away.

                                        CUT TO:

EXT—PINEY WOODS—NIGHT
The group stares at Sam.

>   SAM
>   (picking at the dried
>   blood on his shirt)
>   I had to stop to rest an' when I did, I just . . .
>   I reckon I dozed off.
>   (pause)
>   When I woke up I started walkin' again
>   and seen the fire.

>   CLEVE
>   Mr. Lanham done kilt hisself?

>   ALEX
>   It beats all.

>   DICK
>   It's passin' strange. Don't matter how
>   many times you tell it, it's passin'
>   strange.

>   WILLA
>   (studying Sam)
>   Sam—didjoo' know yer Daddy?

Dick immediately shoots Willa a nonverbal rebuke. Willa half
shrugs and rephrases her question.

>   WILLA
>   (continuing)
>   Do you 'member him?

>   SAM
>   Yes, mam.
>   (pause)
>   *No.*

SAM (CONT'D)
But I try to.

ALEX
(to Sam)
Whatcha' make of Mr. Lanham
Shootin' hisself?

SAM
I heard it much as saw it. Scared me
. . . and I wuz already plenny scared.

Alex nods and looks at Dick. Dick shakes his head.

SAM
(continuing)
Thought sure they wuz comin' to get
me.
(short pause)
I limped away. Fell down. Limped
some more. I kept lookin' back. But after
Mr. Lanham . . .
(long pause)
They jus' didn't come.

ALEX
(facetiously)
Why couldn't Wirt Simms shoot hisself?

Sam doesn't say anything.

DICK
(to Sam)
You got away. Then you made it back
here.

SAM
Yessir.

                    DICK
        That's the important thang. You got
        away. No matter how ennything else
        figures.

                                        JUMP CUT:

EXT—PINEY WOODS—NIGHT
The black folks on the periphery of the group are less active now.
Many are now seated closer to the campfire.

Dick turns to Willa. She notes his attention, cocks her head and
raises her eyebrows.

                    DICK
        You ready, Miss Willa?

                    WILLA
        I reckon, Mr. Richard.

Dick grins.

                    WILLA
                 (continuing)
        Funny world to spend too long in.
        Don'tcha thaink?

Dick nods.

                    CLEVE
        How old you, Miss Willa?

                    WILLA
        Seventy and three.

Willa looks at Sam and then Dick.

WILLA (CONT'D)
(continuing)
I knowed Mr. Lanham since he a
baby.

Sam stares off. Dick shakes his head almost imperceptibly.

WILLA
(continuing)
Lovin' child. We worked on his
folks' place till we was freed.

CUT TO:

MEDIUM CLOSE—PINEY WOODS—CONTINUOUS
Willa wrings her hands and then holds them out toward the fire to
warm them.

WILLA
Crazy world, now. This and that.
(short pause)
We don't say these things anymore, I
know. I knows that. But Mr. Lanham,
he nurse at my breast like my own babies.
(shakes her head)
Crazy to say, I reckon. I know. Even
now, even now. It pain me to hear he
dead, how he dead. Glad ya' got away,
Sam. Mighty glad. Cain't believe a man
who fed at my bosom mixed up in this
sinfulness, this evil.
(pause)
Crazy world. This and that.

CUT TO:

EXT—PINEY WOODS—CONTINUOUS
The group listens intently. Willa's words linger.

DICK

"Crazy" the right word.

WILLA

Sorry. I had'ta tell it how it wuz.

DICK

I know, Miss Willa. This may be the
last time. We gots'ta all tell it.

Willa rubs her hands and places them back in her lap.

WILLA

When I most uh y'all's years, I never
thought I ever have my own cabin. Or
my own cows. Or even be able to walk
down a street in town. It beats all. Lot
changed after the war. Wuz better and
then worse. And then better. And now
a sure sight worse again.
(short pause)
My Harrell—my husband. We marry
just a'fore war. He was a good man.
We had a good life, as living goes.

DICK

I knew him years back.

CUT TO:

MEDIUM CLOSE—PINEY WOODS—CONTINUOUS
Willa crosses her arms and remembers.

WILLA

Yeh, he gone now. Ten-year ago. He
knew Mr. Lanham, too. Called him
Lanny til the day he passed on.
(short pause)
Ennyway.

Willa nods and sits for a minute.

                    WILLIA
                  (continuing)
        They found me out at our cabin. Lil'
        place cozy up in the forest not far south
        uh' here. I heard shootin' all that mornin'
        but didn't get what it wuz all uh-bout . . .
        Some days it rains pellets. Somebody's
        always shootin' 'bout somethin' 'round
        here.
                    (pause)
        Then Ol' Sanchez came by.

                                        CUT TO:

EXT—FRONT STOOP OF WILLA'S CABIN—DAY
Willa is standing on the front stoop of her little cabin swatting at
a spider web (hanging from a tree overhead) with a long thin
branch. After she's done, she drops the branch on a woodpile next
to the stoop.

SANCHEZ, a fifty- or sixty-something-year-old Hispanic man
walks up with a mule that he is leading by a short rope.

                    SANCHEZ
        Meess Wee-la. Meess Wee-la.

                    WILLA
                  (slowly turning)
        Lord gave me two ears, Sanchez—that
        don't mean you gotta' call me twice.
        Howdy!
                  (noticing the mule)
        Whatcha' bring Gwappo for?

                    SANCHEZ
        Me an' Guapo vamos, Meess Wee-la.

WILLA
Vamos? Whut for?

SANCHEZ
Meess Wee-la—Los gringos haff El
Diablo een dem. Los gringos *se han
vuelto locos!*

WILLA
Say it plain, Sanchez. *Plain.*

SANCHEZ
Los gringos, dey loose dey cabezas—
(pointing at his head)
Dey heads!

WILLA
What? Whatcha' sayin?

SANCHEZ
Dey *kee-ling* evvvy-juan.

WILLA
They killin' folks?!

SANCHEZ
Si, Meess Wee-la. Dey kee-leeng
personas de raza negra!

WILLA
They killin' black folk?! That whut all
the shootin' about?

SANCHEZ
Si, Meess Wee-la.

WILLA
That ain't nuthin' new. They been
Killin' us fer years.

WILLA (CONT'D)
(short pause)
Whatchoo' leavin' for?

SANCHEZ
(holds up his arm)
Dey shoot San-chase.

Sanchez has a flesh wound in his left arm.

WILLA
You awright?

SANCHEZ
Si, amiga.

Sanchez holds his arm up and shakes it as if shaking off the wound.

Willa and Sanchez hear gunshots in the distance. Guapo starts, but Sanchez runs his hands along Guapo's neck and he calms.

SANCHEZ
(continuing)
Vamos, Meess Wee-la. *Vamos*.

Willa looks in the direction of the gunfire and shrugs her shoulders.

WILLA
You go, Sanchez. I ain't leavin'.

SANCHEZ
Porque, amiga?

WILLA
Too ol', my friend. *Viejo*. And plain tuckered.

SANCHEZ
Pero—

CUT TO:

EXT—FRONT STOOP OF CABIN—CONTINUOUS
Willa stares at Sanchez.

WILLA
(interrupting)
I'm *bueno*, amigo. Me *bueno*.
(short pause)
Ya' got food? *Comida?*
(motioning to her mouth)
Necessita comida?

CUT TO:

EXT—WILLA'S CABIN—CONTINUOUS
Sanchez smiles.

SANCHEZ
No, amiga.

Sanchez doesn't know what else to say.

SANCHEZ
(continuing)
Te extranare amiga mia.

WILLA
(not understanding
literally, but understanding)
Me, too, Sanchez. Me, too.

Sanchez and Guapo go on.

Willa watches them for a moment and then sits down in a rocking
chair on her front stoop.

Willa hears gunshots again and they are much closer. She begins to rock.

JUMP CUT:

EXT—FRONT STOOP OF CABIN—CONTINUOUS
Willa is still rocking in her rocking chair. A dozen white men appear, half on foot and half on horseback. They all have sacks over their heads, some potato, some cloth (with eyeholes cut in).

Willa regards them quietly—and then starts to laugh. Her laugh is full-throated and true.

CUT TO:

EXT—FRONT STOOP OF CABIN—CONTINUOUS
As Willa guffaws, the sack-headed white men look at one another and back at Willa.

SACKHEAD #1
(humorlessly)
Whatchoo' laughin' at Nee-gress.

CUT TO:

EXT—WILLA'S CABIN—CONTINUOUS
Willa continues to laugh, stops and then laughs again.

WILLA
Sorry. Sorry.
(giggles)
Sorry. It's juss' those masks—
(laughs again)
Make me think potato harvest come
twice this year.

Willa laughs again. Some of the masked men laugh with her.

SACKHEAD #2
HA-HA, *Nigger.*

WILLA
HA-HA, yerself, *Sack-man.*
(wipes her eyes
and composes herself)
Whatcha' want? Come to it.

Willa's uppity, confrontational tone surprises some of the masked men. They hesitate.

CUT TO:

EXT—CABIN'S FRONT STOOP—CONTINUOUS
Willa is emboldened.

WILLA
(continuing)
I done heard tell uh yer deviltry, the
vile killin'—but I ain't gonna run. I
don't have'ta. This is *my* house. I ain't
even gonna hide in it. And I ain't
gonna beg for my life. You is monsters.
One and all . . . and I ain't gonna bow
to ya' or for ya'. You thank those masks
hide who ya' are? You thank they hides
what you all been doin' from the eyes of
the Lord?!

CUT TO:

EXT—IN FRONT OF WILLA'S CABIN—CONTINUOUS
The masked men stare at Willa.

SACKHEAD #1
Awful sassie, Mammie.

SACKHEAD #2
That may be the most ah' ever heard
a negra' talk.

SACKHEAD #1
They can string a few words together
when they git goin', cain't they?

SACKHEAD #2
'Fore they get *strung* up anyway.

WILLA
(eyeballing Sackhead #2)
Ya' don't scare me, Lester Green.

SACKHEAD #1
Whoa, Lester. She knows who you are.

WILLA
(regarding Sackhead #1)
Yes, I do, *Rory Simms*. I got you,
too.

Rory removes his mask. He is a younger version of his father,
Wirt.

SACKHEAD #1
Thought callin' ya' "Mammie" might
throw ya' off, Miss Willa.

WILLA
It didn't, boy. Ya' daddy know ya' out
here killin' folks?

SACKHEAD #1
We ain't out here killin' *folks*—we out
here killin' niggers.

WILLA
I'm sure ya' mama and daddy is shoutin'
proud.

SACKHEAD #2
How come you ain't scared, Negress?
Sassin' us, talkin' outta' place.

WILLA
Hmmph.
(short pause)
Cause I back down to yer kind all my
life, best I knew how, best I could. Had
to. Had to, to protect the ones I cared for,
the ones I loved.
(short pause)
I don't have to mind whut you boys
thank now. One's I love, they gone
or far 'nuff 'way you cain' hurt 'em.

WILLA (CONT'D)
I kin stick my thumb in yer eye now
and twist it. I can laff away—*and you
can't take that away*. I'm done past
carin.'

Sackhead #1 and Sackhead #2 look at one another.

WILLA
(continuing)
I ain't gonna' run. And you ain't gonna'
put a hole in my back.
(pause)
Crazy world, this and that. Grown white
boys 'fraid to come down here and show
they face. Scared of they ol' Auntie.
(smirks)
Right proud, yer folks must be.
Right proud.

SACKHEAD #1
Earl?

Earl (one of the other masked white men on a horse) looks
over at Sackhead #1.

EARL
Yeah, Rory?

SACKHEAD #1
(never looking at
Earl or Willa)
Shoot that bitch.

Earl gets off his horse and walks over to Willa's front stoop. He
draws his pistol and aims it at her.

Willa's smirk becomes a smile. She continues to rock, smiling
at Rory.

Earl shoots Willa and she falls out of her chair, landing on her side.

CLOSE ON: Willa's face. She never stops smiling.

MATCH CUT:

EXT—PINEY WOODS—NIGHT
CLOSE ON: Willa's face. She is still smiling.

Dick, Alex and Sam smile with her.

> DICK
> *Thunderation*, Miss Willa. You got some mighty thick bark on you!

> CLEVE
> You crazy.

> ALEX
> She told 'em, that's all. I think Rory Simms' daddy the one who started all this. He turn beet red when Uncle Abe show up at his house and summon him for county road fixin' day. Big Willie said he done seen smoke come outta' Wirt Simms' ears.

> DICK
> Wirt Simms is a hateful man.

> ALEX
> His boy is a spiteful, backstabbin' peckerwood, just like his daddy.

Cleve and Sam laugh. Dick does not.

> WILLA
> Crazy world.

SAM
(looking at Willa)
This and that.

WILLA
(looking back at Sam)
This and that. I thought that was the
end of me. Went to sleep and didn't
think I'd never wake. But a few hours
later my eyes opened and I sat up.

Willa takes her stick and pokes at the fire again.

WILLA
(continuing)
Lotta' blood, but still had breath. Still
had my breath.

CUT TO:

INT—VENIR RESIDENCE, MORNING—PRESENT DAY
LUTHER sits in the living room napping in a cheap, worn
recliner--his favorite. His, chihuahua, Josie, sits in his lap, also
asleep.

Luther's full head of hair is snow white and his light brown skin
is wrinkled with age; he is 106 years old.

Luther's great-granddaughter, CLEO, enters the living room at
a run, but slows when she sees Luther asleep.

Josie wakes up. Cleo walks over and pets him. Luther slowly
wakes. He opens his eyes without moving.

LUTHER
Whatcha' doin, Cleo?

CLEO
Petting Josie, Granpa.

LUTHER
I know he like that.

Cleo continues to pet Josie.

CLEO
Granpa?

LUTHER
Yes, darlin.'

CLEO
Mama says we're going to a bad place
tomorrow.

LUTHER
Does she?

CLEO
Yes, sir.

LUTHER
(holding out his arms
to get a hug)
Why you reckon your Mama say a
thing like that?

CLEO
(hugging her Grandpa)
I don't know.

LUTHER
(letting Cleo go, but
looking into her eyes)
Ain't no such thing as bad places—just
bad people.
(short pause)
Most of them bad people there are gone
or as old as me. We run into each other,

LUTHER (CONT'D)
I don't think any uh' us in much shape to
do a thing about it.
(long pause)
Your Mama afraid?

CLEO
I don't know, Granpa.
(short pause)
Are you ever afraid?

LUTHER
Ho. I reckon not, not now. I'm too ol'
to be afraid.

CLEO
I wish I was old.

LUTHER
(laughs)
No you don't, girl. Whole world in
front of ya. *Whole life.*

CUT TO:

EXT—PINEY WOODS—NIGHT
The men around the campfire watch Willa.

DICK
I declare, Miss Willa. You only one
I know—*man, woman, Yankee, Apache*—
only one I know or ever heard of talk to a
white man like that and live to tell the tale.

Willa continues to poke at the fire.

WILLA
They got an earful.
(pause)

WILLA (CONT'D)
I sure miss my rockin' chair, though.

Cleve gets up and places another log on the fire.
John groans in his sleep.

DICK
I reckon it's my turn, now.

ALEX
Yep. And Rae next.

JEFF
And then me.

RAE
I don't wanna go next.

DICK
It'll be yer turn.

Rae does not respond.

DICK
(continuing)
They be here soon.

SAM
How you know?

DICK
I done told ya.

CLEVE
He seent 'em.

JOHN
(never opening his eyes)
I seent 'em.

ALEX

John?

Dick waits for John to expound, but John remains silent.

Dick rubs the back of his neck and turns to the fire.

DICK

It was later when they got to us. One
of them mobs got my Daddy on his
way back from fishin' the creek
that mornin.'
(looks at Jeff)
Jeff found him and come an' got me.
We took him to that big cypress
close to the house to bury him. We'd
heard the stories and we was never
outta' earshot of all the shootin'. But I
didn't want my Daddy messed with.
(long pause)
Didn't hear 'em at first. We just
finished coverin' up Daddy and they
wuz on us sudden-like.

CUT TO:

EXT—GRAVE UNDER CYPRESS TREE—AFTERNOON
Dick and Jeff have just finished covering up the grave of Dick's
father. Two dozen white men, led by Wirt, approach. Drew is no
longer with them.

Wirt is still on horseback, his shotgun at the ready. Dick hears
them and turns to face Wirt.

DICK

(under his breath)
Stay behind me, Jeffrey.

JEFF
Yes, sir.

DICK
(feigning courtesy)
Hullo, Wirt. How you doin'?

WIRT
(matching Dick's
affectation)
Howdy, Dick. Grand, sir. Mighty fine,
if I do say so muhself.

DICK
(nonchalantly)
Can I help you with something?

WIRT
No, sir. We's here to help you.

DICK
That so?

WIRT
'Spect it is.

DICK
Oh, I think I got it, Wirt. But thanks for
offerin'.

Wirt smiles. Dick does not.

WIRT
Yer welcome, Dick. Yer welcome.
(pause)
You know, Dick . . . I hadn't run
across too many brave niggers
today. I thank they damn near gone
in these parts. There's a word fer it.

WIRT (CONT'D)
(turning to the other
white men)
What's the word fer it?

Wirt's men look at one another.

MEEKS
(smiling)
Dead?

WIRT
Dead, yeah—but a dead nigger don't
account for much. But a country mile
of dead niggers, there's a fancy word
for that.
(leaning back in
his saddle)
What is that word, Dick?
(short pause)
My Elsie wuz sayin' it the other day.
Blubberin' about some bird somebody
gone and clubbed to death. Kilt the last
one.
(thinking)
Last one and they kilt it dead.

MUNK
Extinct?

WIRT
Egg-stinct! That's the word.
(trying to get a rise
out of Dick)
Brave niggers down here damn near
eggs-stinct. You jus' might be the last
Mohican, Dick.

Dick is unfazed. Wirt changes tacks.

102

WIRT
(continuing)
Ran into yer Daddy earlier.

DICK
(clenching his shovel
handle more tightly)
That right?

WIRT
That's right.

Dick's features are stone.

WIRT
(continuing)
Yessir, ever-thang wuz awright, 'cept
he had him an empty stringer.
(short pause)
Fish not bitin' I guess.

Dick holds his tongue.

WIRT
(continuing)
That who yer plantin' this fine, sunny
afternoon?

Wirt stares at Dick. Dick does not answer the question.

WIRT
(continuing)
Tell you what, Dick.

Dick is motionless and mute.

WIRT
(continuing)
No sense in leaving you here to rot.

WIRT (CONT'D)
That wouldn't be very neighborly.
How about you an' yer boy dig two
more graves and we'll plant you two
beside 'im?
(thumps his hat farther
back on his head)
Hell, I might even say a word or two.

DICK
(swinging the shovel)
Run Jeffrey!

Dick launches the shovel at Wirt. Jeff drops his shovel and runs.

CUT TO:

EXT—NEXT TO BIG CYPRESS TREE—AFTERNOON
Wirt ducks to avoid the hurled shovel and falls completely off his
horse. Meeks shoots Dick in the back with his rifle and Dick
collapses face first.

Jeff escapes.

CUT TO:

EXT—GRAVE AT CYPRESS TREE—AFTERNOON
Dick tries to raise up and Meeks shoots him again.

CUT TO:

EXT—NEXT TO BIG CYPRESS TREE—AFTERNOON
Wirt gets up furious. He empties his pistol in the direction Jeff
fled and then re-holsters it.

Wirt grabs the shovel and walks towards Dick.

CUT TO:

EXT—GRAVE UNDER CYPRESS TREE—AFTERNOON
Dick's whole body shakes as he tries to lift himself again;
Wirt hits him over the head with the shovel twice.

                                              MATCH CUT:

EXT—PINEY WOODS—NIGHT
Dick rubs the back of his neck. Jeff wipes away the tears in his
eyes. Alex and Sam exchange glances and Willa shakes her
head.

                          DICK
                I'd like to say I worked those boys
                over. But I cain't. Wasn't that way
                a'tall.
                          (short pause)
                That shovel put me out.

                          WILLA
                Your daddy was a fine man.

                          ALEX
                He wuz, Dick.

                          DICK
                Wirt Simms.

                          ALEX
                Wirt Simms.

                          SAM
                This and that.

                          DICK
                This and that.

CLOSE ON: Dick's face. He looks tired.

                                              DISSOLVE TO:

INT—HOLLIE-JAWAID STUDY, PRESENT DAY— NIGHT

CLOSE ON: Constance's face. She's all grown up, and she looks tired.

Constance is sitting at a desk, studying a small stack of newspaper clippings. The headlines read "Race Riot in East Texas," "Bloody Race War" and "Two Dozen Dead."

Her husband, SHEREYAR, a sturdy light-skinned man, comes in.

> SHEREYAR
> What are you doing, babe?

> CONSTANCE
> I can't sleep.

> SHEREYAR
> It's 2 a.m.
> (rubs his eyes)
> You gotta get some rest.

> CONSTANCE
> I know.

> SHEREYAR
> You coming to bed soon?

> CONSTANCE
> Yes, babe.
> (pause)
> You know how much this means to me.

> SHEREYAR
> Yes, of course.

> CONSTANCE
> I'll be right there.

Shereyar leaves the room. Constance stares after him and then
returns her attention to the collection of faded newspaper
clippings on the desk.

CUT TO:

EXT—PINEY WOODS—NIGHT
Dick and the rest of the small group around the campfire stare at
the flames.

> ALEX
> Whatcha' thaink set the white folks
> off?

> DICK
> I cain't rightly say.

> WILLA
> I thank it just in they nature. If they
> see somebody else got's it, they try
> to git it.

> SAM
> But whut we got?

> WILLA
> A good life. *Our own life.*
> (short pause)
> Here in these parts, we have it good
> for our-selfs. Dick's people got land.
> Alex's family got land, a fine granary
> and a bustlin' general mercantile. We
> got land and cabins and shade. Lot's
> uh shade in the forests. And water real
> close. Not ever-thaing outta' the Sears
> and Roebuck, mind you. But we don't
> want for much. We have things alright.
> Even got a black girl college down the
> road near Grapeland.

WILLA (CONT'D)
(pause)
Some white folks, they just cain't stand
to see us makin' our way. It's simple
as that.

SAM
It ain't right.

ALEX
What *right* got to do with it? *They
white*.

DICK
That's the way of it. That's how it
shakes out.

The campfire group is momentarily silent again.

DICK
(continuing, without
looking in Rae's direction)
Rae?

Rae remains silent.

DICK
Rae.

Tears begin streaming down Rae's cheeks. She sobs.

WILLA
(holding her arms out)
C'mere girl.

Rae steps over to Willa and sits next to her on the tree stump.
Willa puts her arm around Rae and pulls her close.

CUT TO:

EXT—GAS STATION, PRESENT DAY—NIGHT
TUCSON, a young black man in his late twenties, former-military, is pumping gas into his truck. His dark skin is ashen under the gas station's yellowing fluorescent lights.

Tuscon's darker-skinned 10-year-old son, STAN, sticks his head out the driver's side window.

> TUCSON
> What's up, little man?

> STAN
> We almost there, Daddy?

> TUCSON
> Not yet, buddy. Not yet.
> (finishes pumping gas)
> Tired?

> STAN
> Yes, sir.

> TUCSON
> Get some more sleep, son. We'll be there soon.

CUT TO:

EXT—EAST TEXAS FOREST—NIGHT
Willa and Rae are sitting on the tree stump together.

> WILLA
> It's awwright, child. It's awwright.

> RAE
> It ain't.

> WILLA
> Tell it, girl. It'll help.

110

                         ALEX
         We with you, Rae.

                          SAM
         We here, Rae.

Rae looks at Alex and Sam.

                         CLEVE
         I didn't wanna either, Rae. But I feel
         better. We together.

Rae looks at Dick and wipes her eyes. Rae looks up at Willa and
Willa nods.

                          RAE
         Well, I don't . . .

Rae sniffs and looks at the ground and then stares at the fire.

                          RAE
                     (continuing)
         Truth is, there's a place for me in there.

Sam and Cleve exchange concerned glances. Alex looks to Willa.

                         WILLA
         Why, that's foolish, child. Ain't yer
         place to say. Ain't yer place to know.

                          RAE
         I know. *I know.*

                         WILLA
         How you know?

                          RAE
                (tears stream down her cheeks)
         I loss my baby.

CUT TO:

EXT—PINEY WOODS—AFTERNOON
Two white men on horses, and a dozen white men on foot, move
through the woods.

CUT TO:

INT—CABIN IN PINEY WOODS—AFTERNOON
Rae is sitting on a stool next to a homemade, wooden rocking
crib, rocking a light-skinned baby who she affectionately calls
SPIDER.

Rae's boyfriend, DANIEL, a resourceful, wiry black man in his
early twenties, is standing close to her.

Rae's grandfather, JEBIDIAH, an ancient, almost Australian-
aboriginal-looking black man wearing an equally ancient, fraying
topcoat, is sitting in a crooked chair next to the fireplace.

> DANIEL
> Somethin' goin' on.
> (pause)
> I was working the creek bottom on
> the Mortenson spread and Fleck
> Taylor run up and tell that folks
> Gittin' shot from Mound City to
> Denson Springs. He say no rhyme,
> no reason. He say he leavin.'

> JEBIDIAH
> I heard some shootin'.

> RAE
> Who shootin' who?

> DANIEL
> Fleck say white folks whiskied up
> and loaded for bear. He say they heard

112

DANIEL (CONT'D)
there was a risin' and come this way to
put it down.

JEBIDIAH
Risin'? T'weren't no risin' down here.

DANIEL
Tell me. I know.

RAE
Whatta' we do?

DANIEL
Hide. Or run, maybe.

RAE
What about Spider?

Daniel doesn't say anything. He turns towards the fire.

Jebidiah also remains silent. Rae senses Daniel's frustration
and smiles faintly.

RAE
(continuing)
I carry him.
(picking Spider up and
looking into his eyes)
He don't weigh nothin'.

Daniel, Rae and Jebidiah hear a noise in the woods outside the
cabin.

CUT TO:

EXT—CABIN IN PINEY WOODS—AFTERNOON
White men approach the cabin and spread out in front of it.

CUT TO:

INT—CABIN IN PINEY WOODS—AFTERNOON
Rae lies Spider on the only decent bed in the cabin and ties a
colorful bandanna around her head. Daniel peers out through a
small, vertical slit in the front cabin wall. He sees the white men
taking position.

> DANIEL
> We way late.

> JEBIDIAH
> White folk?

> DANIEL
> Thick as picket fence.

> RAE
> What we do?

> DANIEL
> I'll take out towards the Birdsong shack.
> You two sit still a couple of breaths and
> make towards that horse briar on the
> trail to Augusta. I meet you there.

> RAE
> Daniel—

SMASH CUT:

EXT—CABIN IN PINEY WOODS—AFTERNOON
The white men begin firing into the cabin.

The barrage lasts several seconds.

When the shots subside, Daniel appears out from behind the
cabin, running left. He tears through the brush and most of
the white men on foot, and one on horseback, follow him.

114

It was a diversionary tactic.

As the remaining white men on foot and the other white man on horseback are reloading, Rae and Jebidiah appear out from behind the cabin running right.

The residual group of white men finishes reloading and begins to fire on them.

JEBIDIAH
Run, Rae. Run!

Rae is moving faster than Jebidiah.

Jebidiah jogs a short distance behind and then turns to face their attackers, shielding Rae's flight.

JEBIDIAH
(continuing)
Naah-sir, massa. Naah-sir. *Please* sir.

A bullet strikes Jebidiah in the leg and he drops to one knee.

A white man on horseback sets after Jebidiah and Rae. Two white men on foot follow.

Jebidiah pulls a rag out of his pocket and holds it against his leg wound. The white man on the horse approaches him.

JEBIDIAH
(continuing)
It's awright. T'wuddn't nothin'. Please
massa, sir. Please—

The white man on horseback rushes past Jebidiah, ignoring him.

JEBIDIAH
(continuing)
Nothin'' sir . . . nothin' at all.

JEBIDIAH (CONT'D)
(louder)
Nothin'.

The two white men on foot reach Jebediah.

JEBIDIAH
(continuing)
Please master, sir . . . *Please.*

The two white men on foot beat Jebidiah unconscious.

JUMP CUT:

**EXT—FARTHER OUT IN PINEY WOODS—
AFTERNOON**
As the gallop of the white man's horse bears down on Rae, she
continues to run, clutching the infant close.

A tree limb catches the bandanna tied around Rae's hair and
removes it, spinning her around.

Spun around, Rae sees a white man on horseback closing fast.
She turns and begins running again.

JUMP CUT:

EXT—FARTHER OUT IN WOODS—AFTERNOON
The white man on horseback catches Rae. She slows to a walk
but does not look back. CLOSE ON: Rae's face.

DISSOLVE TO:

INT—VENIR RESIDENCE, PRESENT DAY—NIGHT
CLOSE ON: Luther's face. Luther looks lost. He is standing
in the living room, leaning on the cane in his right hand.
Luther's granddaughter, CORINA, a curvy black woman in her
early forties, comes in through the front door,

CORINA
Grandaddy. You ready to go?

LUTHER
I reckon. Where we goin'?

CORINA
Well, if you've already forgot, maybe
we can go somewhere else.

LUTHER
I ain't forgot.
            (short pause)
We're goin' home.

CORINA
            (laughs)
You're going home. I'm from Memphis.
            (pause)
We're taking you. We're taking you
home.
            (locking her right arm
            around Luther's left)
Everybody else is in the truck. You
ready?

LUTHER
Can I take Josie?

CORINA
He's already in the truck. Cleo has him.

LUTHER
Okay. I'm ready.

Corina guides Luther out of the living room and through the front
door.

                                        CUT TO:

117

EXT—FARTHER OUT IN PINEY WOODS—AFTERNOON
Rae is still walking. The white man on the horse is behind her,
matching her pace.

Thinking of running again, Rae looks left and then right. There is
no cover. She knows she will not get far.

Rae continues to walk. The white man on the horse follows.

CUT TO:

INT—VENIR EXCURSION—NIGHT
Luther, Corina and Cleo are all seated in a Ford Excursion and
Corina's husband, Bedford, a heavyset black man in his early
forties, is behind the wheel. Josie is asleep on Luther's lap. Cleo
is asleep in her seat.

Luther dozes in and out in his seat.

> BEDFORD
> (looking at Luther in
> his rearview mirror)
> How long's it been since you went
> back, Luther?

> LUTHER
> (eyes opening)
> Oh . . . Long time, coming up on a
> century, I reckon. Visited once when
> I's real young, 'bout Cleo's age. But we
> Didn't dilly-dally . . . our name was mud.
> We passed through on our way to Kirvin.
> My daddy had family there. He share-
> cropped awhile . . . and I started helpin'
> him when I's 'bout six.

> CORINA
> How old were you when you left Kirvin?

118

LUTHER

I's eleven, I think. Mebbe twelve. We
skedaddled when those folks burnt those
three boys at the stake.
(pondering)
Terrible bizness—middle of the
night. We just up and left.

BUFORD

They burned three people at the
stake?

LUTHER

Yes, sir. Sure as yer sittin'there. Three
black boys, burned to a crisp.
(looks out the window)
I ain't been back to East Texas since.

CORINA

Sure you still wanna' go?

LUTHER

Yes, ma'am. Yes, ma'am.
(long pause)
Things they did to us . . . You
wouldn't believe.
(pause)
Don't even seem real, now. Don't
even seem possible. But they done
'em. They done 'em all. They
happened. And now they's somebody
down there sayin' they happened—
admittin' they happened. I'm goin'
even if I gotta' walk.

CUT TO:

EXT—FARTHER OUT IN THE WOODS—AFTERNOON
Rae suddenly stops walking and faces her pursuer. He stops

his horse a few steps away.

Rae's attempt to affect fierce determination abruptly fades. She
recognizes her pursuer.

RAE

You.

Rae's pursuer does not respond.

RAE
(continuing)

You.

Rae nibbles at her lip and shakes her head.

Rae opens the blanket to reveal Spider's face. She turns the infant
toward the white man.

RAE
(continuing)

Look at 'im. Ya' took me in the
marsh when I wuz goin' home after
workin' yer daddy's fields.
(short pause)
I never tole no one.
(eyes welling up)
What good it'uh done?
(wiping her eyes)
Ya' give me this little boy my
family, my man—he know ain't his.
(tears begin streaming
down her cheeks)
Why dintcha' jus' shoot me?
(raising her voice)
Why dintcha' just shoot me then?

The white pursuer regards Rae and the baby silently. The two
white men on foot approach in the distance.

                              RAE
                          (continuing)
                    Look at him. His skin yers more'n
                    mine.

Rae looks at her son and then back up at his father.

The white man raises his gun and Rae turns to the baby. Rae
smiles through her tears.

The white man hesitates for one beat and shoots Rae. She falls—
but is careful not to drop her boy.

The two white men on foot arrive. The baby begins to cry.

The white man on the horse turns and rides off.

One of the white men on foot attempts to pull Rae's baby away.
She fights to hold him, but she is growing weak. The baby cries.

One of the white men on foot grabs the barrel of his shotgun
with both hands and smashes Rae over the head with the butt.

The baby cries and Rae loses consciousness.

                                                    CUT TO:

EXT—PINEY WOODS—NIGHT
Rae has her hands up as if she is still trying to hold on to her son.
Feeling helpless, the men in the group watch her sadly.

Willa wipes her teary eyes and pulls Rae's reaching arms down.
Willa hugs Rae closer.

                              WILLA
                    It's alright, child. Nuthin' you coulda'
                    done. Nuthin' anybody coulda' done.

                              122

                          WILLA
          It's alright, child. Nuthin' you coulda'
          done. Nuthin' anybody coulda' done.

                          ALEX
          Rae?

Rae turns to Alex blankly.

                          ALEX
                     (softening his
                        voice)
          Rae?

                          RAE
                      (blankly)
          Yes.

                          ALEX
          Didja' ever find him?

                          RAE
                      (blankly)
          Who?

                          ALEX
          Your boy?

Rae doesn't answer.

Willa gets Alex's attention non-verbally and shakes her head,
indicating Alex should leave it alone.

Rae wipes her eyes absently.

                          RAE
          We called him Spider. He grab stuff. He
          Just a baby but he grab stuff and hang on.

SAM

We get out uh this, we'll find him.

CLEVE

First thang we do.

ALEX

We get 'im back, Rae. First thang.

RAE

First thang?

DICK

First thang.

CUT TO:

INT—CONSTANCE'S BEDRM, PRESENT DAY—NIGHT
Constance and Shereyar are in bed. Shereyar is asleep but
Constance is awake.

The clock beside the bed says 5:30 a.m. and begins to beep.
Constance turns it off and sits up.

Constance gets out of the bed and opens the bedroom closet door.
She grabs a box off a high shelf, takes it over to the bed and sits
in the bed with it. She turns on a bedside lamp and takes the lid
off the box.

The box is full of pictures. Constance begins thumbing through
them and setting them aside.

Constance smiles at a few of the pictures, but sets them
aside like the rest.

After a few moments, Constance comes across the photo she's
looking for. She smiles at it, and then looks sad. She holds it to
her heart and puts the rest of the pictures back in the box.

EXT—PINEY WOODS—NIGHT
The small group around the campfire is tired and weary. Cleve
yawns. John groans.

>   DICK
>   Almost time.

>   ALEX
>   You been sayin' that for a spell, now.

>   DICK
>   Gittin' close. Gittin' close.

>   SAM
>   But how you know?

>   DICK
>   I toldja.' I seen 'em.

>   ALEX
>   Who?

Dick doesn't answer immediately.

>   DICK
>   Don't be gettin' your hackles up. They
>   Comin'. They be here soon.

>   WILLA
>   Lord, I hope so.

>   DICK
>   You'll see. Soon.

INT—TUCSON'S TRUCK, PRESENT DAY—NIGHT
Tucson drives. His son Stan is still awake.

STAN
Where we going, Daddy?

TUCSON
(lost in thought)
We're going home.

STAN
We're going back home already?

TUCSON
No.
(smiles)
Not our house. Our people's home. Where
we come from.
(pause)
Way back.

STAN
Way back?

TUCSON
Waaayyy back.

STAN
Where's that?

TUCSON
Texas.

STAN
Texas?!

TUCSON
Yes, sir. Our people are from Texas.
But something happened there . . . so
they went away.

STAN

Texas is where the Alamo is.

TUCSON

Yes, it is.

STAN

Did our people fight in the Alamo?

TUCSON
(laughs)

No.
(thinks for a moment)
No. They fought in a different Alamo.

STAN

Really?

TUCSON

Really.

STAN

Were our people brave, Daddy?

TUCSON

Yes.
(sneaking a serious,
earnest gaze at his boy)
Our people were the bravest folks that
ever lived.

CUT TO:

EXT—PINEY WOODS—NIGHT
Alex stretches. Dick smiles at Willa and Willa grins. Rae stares
blankly.

DICK

You ready, Jeffrey?

                    JEFF
Yessir.

                    DICK
Tell us, son. Tell us what happened.

                    JEFF
Yessir. You tole me to run and I did. I run.

                    DICK
Only thing I could do, son. Only
thing you could do. *And you got away.*

                    JEFF
I got away. One uh' those shotgun
blasts peppered me pretty good, but
I got away.

                    ALEX
That buckshot stings.

                    JEFF
It do. It do. But I didn't stop runnin'.

                                    CUT TO:

EXT—PINEY WOODS—EARLY EVENING
Jeff is running. He passes through a break in the woods and
another group of white men fire on him.

Jeff changes direction immediately and keeps going. A bullet
grazes him in the side, but he keeps moving.

                                    JUMP CUT:

EXT—PINEY WOODS NEAR CREEK—EARLY EVENING
Jeff hears gunshots in the distance, but keeps running. He
approaches a creek and slows down.

CUT TO:

EXT—PINEY WOODS CREEK—EARLY EVENING
Jeff goes to the edge and gets down on his hands and knees. He lowers his head and takes a quick drink and then a longer drink.

Jeff gets back up and starts to jog off. He sees a body farther down, also at the water's edge.

Jeff starts to ignore the body and go on, but he changes his mind and kneels. He listens for a moment, to make sure no else is around.

CUT TO:

EXT—FARTHER DOWN CREEK—EARLY EVENING
Approaching slowly, Jeff discovers a little black girl lying near the creek's edge, her head in the water. She has no evident gunshot wounds, but her fingers and hands are caked with mud and it is obvious that she has clawed at the muddy dirt along the bank.

It appears someone happened upon her getting a drink and simply held her head under the water.

Jeff's eyes well up and he covers his mouth with his hands.

Jeff breaks into a run again.

CUT TO:

INT—CONSTANCE'S CAR, PRESENT DAY—MORNING
Shereyar is driving. Constance stares out the window. The Dallas skyline appears in Shereyar's rear-view mirror.

Constance turns to Shereyar as if to say something but doesn't. She stares at the road ahead and her eyes well up.

Constance pulls out the picture she retrieved from the box and looks at it. Constance wipes her eyes and unsuccessfully tries to maintain her composure. She begins to sob.

> SHEREYAR
> Babe. What's wrong?

> CONSTANCE
> I . . .
>> (wiping her eyes with some
>> kleenex)
> I'm so . . . *happy.*

> SHEREYAR
>> (laughs)
> Happy!? Then why are you crying?
>> (pause)
> C'mon, baby. Why are you crying?

Constance composes herself.

> CONSTANCE
> I'm happy. But it's been so long. *It's
> taken so long.*
>> (wiping her nose with
>> the kleenex)
> My daddy and my uncle tried for forever,
> and now they're gone. And now it's
> finally happening. I wish they were here.
> We finished what they started. We finally
> Finished, and they're gone.
>> (smiling briefly)
> I wish they were here to see it.

> SHEREYAR
>> (smiling)
> They will be, baby. They will be.

CUT TO:

EXT—MARSH OUT IN THE WOODS—EARLY EVENING
Jeff maneuvers through a marsh. The slog slows him down.

Jeff discovers a black man's body in bloody mud. The muddy hoof prints around the body suggest he was trampled alive or shot and then trampled. Jeff clenches his teeth and moves on.

CUT TO:

EXT—EDGE OF MARSH—EARLY EVENING
Jeff reaches the edge of the marsh and unintentionally comes up on another group of white men. He surprises them and runs.

The white men retrieve their weapons, take hasty aim and start firing. Jeff is hit again, but keeps running.

JUMP CUT:

EXT—PINEY WOODS—EARLY EVENING
Jeff is still moving slowly through the woods. His shirt and britches are coated with blood and his breathing is labored.

Jeff is not watching his path or his surroundings. His wounds render him weak and incautious. He jogs into a clearing and immediately falls into a deep trench.

JUMP CUT:

EXT—DARK TRENCH—LATE EVENING
Jeff is lying on his back, momentarily unconscious. He wakes up disoriented. A putrid odor hits him and he rolls over on his side and dry-wretches twice.

Jeff covers his nose with a shirt-sleeve, leans up on his free elbow and looks around.

The trench Jeff is lying in is approximately ten feet square and six feet deep. The large trees in the deep woods block the moonlight, so visibility is limited.

It takes several moments for Jeff to reorient himself, but when he does, he begins to gasp and scream hoarsely. The trench is filled with dead people. Dead black people.

Wheezing, Jeff struggles to stand up and then starts to rub his eyes as if he might scoop them out of their sockets.

Tears run down Jeff's dirty, bloody cheeks and he moans and whimpers. Jeff screams and then stops, afraid he will be heard. He covers his mouth with both hands, but no one comes.

Jeff composes himself and stands up, stepping around the bodies to the edge of the trench.

CUT TO:

EXT—INTERIOR EDGE OF TRENCH—LATE EVENING
Jeff begins to climb, but he is weak from blood loss. He slides back down in the trench and tries again.

Jeff struggles, eventually making it out of the trench, but he's sobbing uncontrollably.

CUT TO:

EXT—GROUND ABOVE TRENCH—LATE EVENING
Jeff lies on the ground above the trench and covers his mouth with both hands until he stops sobbing. Then his eyes roll back in his head and he loses consciousness.

JUMP CUT:

EXT—EDGE OF DARK TRENCH—LATE EVENING
Jeff wakes slowly and then springs up on his knees. He seems surprised no one has found him. He gets to his feet slowly and peers into the trench.

CUT TO:

POV—LOOKING INTO PIT—LATE EVENING
Jeff sees the bodies of fourteen to sixteen dead black men and women piled up in the trench.

CUT TO:

EXT—GROUND ABOVE TRENCH—LATE EVENING

Jeff stares helplessly. Jeff hears a twig break in the vicinity and starts moving again.

CUT TO:

EXT—PINEY WOODS—NIGHT
Jeff stares into the woods. No one in the campfire group knows what to say.

Sam has his head in his hands. Dick wipes his eyes.

> SAM
> (raising his head)
> Did you know any of them, Jeff?

> JEFF
> It wuz . . . It wuz dark.
> (short pause)
> I tried not to look at their faces. I couldn't.
> I wuz afraid.

> ALEX
> How many you reckon?

> JEFF
> Least a dozen. Mebbe more.

> CLEVE
> What wuz they doin' there?

The sun is beginning to rise in the east. One of its first rays falls on Jeff's cheek.

> JEFF
> I don't rightly know. But I thank white
> folks wuz just dumpin' 'em there.

> CLEVE
> What about they families?

RAE
How will they know?

ALEX
They won't know.
(short pause)
We know.
(short pause)
They wuz hidin' the bodies.

RAE
Why?

ALEX
To git away with it.

WILLA
We cain't let em.

JOHN
(eyes closed)
They got away?

DICK
You back, John?

JOHN
(leaning up, eyes still
closed)
I don't know.

It has begun to get light. Dick stands up.

DICK
It's time.

SAM
They here?

                                DICK
        They're close.
                        (short pause)
        See if you can git John up. We gotta' go
        a little ways farther, git to the edge of the
        forest.

                                CLEVE
        You sure it's alright?

                                DICK
        It's alright. You'll see.

Alex and Jeff help John up, placing each of his arms around their
necks. Willa gets up with Rae. Sam and Cleve follow Dick.

                                SAM
        What about the fire?

                                DICK
                        (nodding at the folks on
                        the periphery)
        Leave it for them. They might need it.
                        (leading the way)
        We come this far. We just need to
        go a little farther.

The campfire group leaves and the unsure folks on the periphery
follow cautiously, several steps behind.

                                                CUT TO:

EXT—PINEY WOODS—EARLY MORNING
The members of the campfire group trudge through the woods.
The folks from the periphery follow.

                                DICK
        Almost there. C'mon.

INT—CONSTANCE'S CAR, PRESENT DAY—MORNING
Shereyar and Constance are deep in the piney woods now.
Shereyar is still behind the wheel. Constance stares out the
window taking in the pine trees as they fly by.

CUT TO:

EXT—EDGE OF PINEY WOODS—MORNING
The campfire group reaches the edge of the forest. The folks
on the periphery linger behind.

ALEX
Where we goin', Dick?

DICK
We here.

JOHN
Where is here?

DICK
You'll see.

The campfire group steps to the edge of the piney woods forest and peer out. John is still supported by Alex and Jeff. Willa is standing with Rae.

CUT TO:

EXT—FARM ROAD, PRESENT DAY—MORNING
Hundreds of African Americans and a few white folks—men, women, children and families—are slowly gathering round a veiled monument.

Luther, Corina, Buford and Cleo stand near the front of the crowd, on one side. Cleo holds Josie.

On the other side of the gathering are Constance and Shereyar and Tucson and Stan. Constance and Shereyar are hugging kinfolk and talking to relatives.

CUT TO:

EXT—EDGE OF PINEY WOODS—MORNING
The campfire group stares at the gathering in amazement and disbelief.

RAE
What's happenin'?

SAM

Who they?

WILLA

Oh my . . .

JEFF

What . . . *Who?*

CLEVE

Is this Heaven?

DICK
(grinning)

They our people.

ALEX

They—*how?* What they wearin?!

Dick smiles.

CUT TO:

EXT—SIDE OF FARM RD, PRESENT DAY—MORNING
The gathering faces the historical marker and sings "Lift Every
Voice."

CUT TO:

EXT—EDGE OF PINEY WOODS—MORNING
The campfire group stands at the edge of the forest, captivated by
the gathering.

JEFF

What they doin'?

DICK

Celebratin'.

ALEX
Celebratin' what?

DICK
Us. They celebratin' us.

CLEVE
But we thought . . .

CUT TO:

EXT—STRETCH OF FM RD, PRESENT DAY—MORNING
A small group of people (including Constance and Luther)
standing near the veiled monument step forward and unveil it.

The gathering cheers and claps. Luther flashes a happy grin
and Constance begins to cry.

CUT TO:

EXT—FARM ROAD, PRESENT DAY—MORNING
CLOSE ON: Slocum Massacre Historical Marker (for audience
to
read).

**RACIAL TENSIONS IN AMERICA IN THE EARLY
TWENTIETH CENTURY WERE SOMETIMES PUNCTUATED
BY VIOLENT OUTBURSTS. ONE SUCH OCCASION BEGAN
NEAR SLOCUM AND DENSON SPRINGS AND SPREAD
ACROSS A WIDE AREA NEAR THE ANDERSON-HOUSTON
COUNTY LINE. BEGIN-NING ON THE MORNING OF JULY 29,
1910, GROUPS OF ARMED WHITE MEN SHOT AND KILLED
AFRICAN AMERICANS, FIRST FIRING ON A GROUP NEAR
SADLER'S CREEK. MURDERS IN THE BLACK COMMUNITY
CONTINUED DURING THE REMAINDER OF THAT DAY AND
NIGHT. ACCOUNTS IN STATE AND NATIONAL
NEWSPAPERS BROUGHT WIDESPREAD ATTENTION TO
THE SITUATION. JUDGES ORDERED SALOONS AND GUN
AND AMMUNITION STORES TO CLOSE, AND THE STATE
MILITIA AND TEXAS RANGERS WERE DISPATCHED TO**

THE AREA. THE MURDERS OF EIGHT MEN WERE OFFICIALLY RECORDED. THE VICTIMS WERE CLEVELAND LARKIN, ALEX HOLLEY, SAM BAKER, DICK WILSON, JEFF WILSON, WILLA CAMPBELL, JOHN HAYS AND RAE THOMPSON. MANY AFRICAN AMERICAN FAMILIES FLED THE AREA AND DID NOT RETURN. ELEVEN WHITE MEN WERE SOON AR-RESTED, AND DISTRICT JUDGE BENJAMIN H. GARDNER EMPANELED A GRAND JURY WITHIN A WEEK. WHEN ITS FINDINGS WERE REPORTED ON AUGUST 17, SEVEN MEN WERE INDICTED. THE CASES WERE MOVED TO HARRIS COUNTY BUT WERE NEVER PROSECUTED. THE EVENTS WHICH CAME TO BE KNOWN AS THE 'SLOCUM MASSACRE' LARGELY DISAPPEARED FROM PUBLIC VIEW IN SUBSEQUENT GENERATIONS.

CUT TO:

EXT—EDGE OF EAST TEXAS FOREST—MORNING
The campfire group looks on in awe and wonder.

RAE
Who is that? What's happenin?

DICK
They did it, Rae. They did it. That monument is for us. *For what was done to us.*

ALEX
They's Holleys out there!

DICK
They's all of us out there. *All of us.*

CLEVE
What happened?

DICK
What happened to us was forgotten.

DICK (CONT'D)
Now the truth of it—it's been tole.
They know the truth.

SAM
But that means we . . . That means we gone.
We gone.

ALEX
Gone?

DICK
Yes. We gone. We been gone. We just
. . . we just didn't know we wuz gone.

RAE
Passed on, *gone?*

DICK
Passed on, gone. Yes.

Dick let's it sink in and then turns his attention to Rae.

DICK
(continuing,
touching Rae's arm)
Rae.

RAE
Yes, Mr. Richard.

DICK
Your baby.

RAE
(still looking at the
marker crowd)
Yeh.

DICK
Spider wuddn't with us back there
at the fire. Right?

RAE
(turning to Dick)
Right. Yes.

DICK
(holding Rae's shoulders
and looking into her
eyes)
Rae—that means he made it. He lived.

RAE
He lived? *He alive!*

DICK
He made it.

SAM
We didn't?

DICK
We didn't. But he did.

RAE
Spider did?

DICK
(releasing Rae and
pointing at the crowd)
They did.

RAE
Who they?

DICK
They yer great-grandbabies, Rae. They

144

DICK (CONT'D)
my great-great-grandbabies. They John
and Pearl's great grandbabies. They
Jeffrey's kin, Cleve's kin, Sam's kin. They
Alex's folks. They Willa's folks. *They us.*

RAE
Can we see them? Can we go out there?

ALEX
(turning to Dick)
We already out there, ain't we?

DICK
Yes, Alex. Our names . . . they on
the monument.

SAM
(looking back at the souls
on the periphery)
What about them?

DICK
They stuck. They's lost. They people
don't know about them yet. They
families don't know they're still here.

WILLA
Crazy world.

CLEVE
Crazy world.

CUT TO:

EXT—FARM ROAD, PRESENT DAY—MORNING
The campfire group leaves the trees at the edge of the forest and
disappears in the crowd.

Constance and Tucson stand teary-eyed near the marker.

Tucson ruffles Stan's hair with his hand. Stan looks up at the sign.

Constance hugs Shereyar.

Tucson picks Stan up and puts him on his shoulders. Tucson steps closer to the sign so Stan can see it.

Stan stares at it momentarily and then looks back at the happy crowd.

                    STAN
                 (wide-eyed)
          Is this our people, Daddy?

                   TUCSON
          This is our people, son.

                    STAN
          This is cray-cray, Daddy.

Tucson chuckles.

The crowd talks about the marker and takes turns standing in front of it to take pictures or get a closer look. Constance and Shereyar approach Tucson and Stan,

                  CONSTANCE
               (looking up at Stan)
             You're awful tall.

Stan laughs. Constance and Shereyar begin talking to Tucson.

Constance sees Luther over Tucson's shoulder and finally recognizes him.

Constance approaches Luther. Shereyar continues talking to

Tucson.

CUT TO:

EXT—FARM ROAD—MORNING
Constance gently grabs Luther's arm and he turns to face her.

> CONSTANCE
> Excuse me, sir, but is your name
> Luther?

> LUTHER
> Yes, mam. It is.

> CONSTANCE
> *Omigosh.* I haven't seen you in . . .

> LUTHER
> Who might you be, ma'am?

> CONSTANCE
> Constance.

> LUTHER
> Constance?
> (thinking)
> Leo's little girl?

> CONSTANCE
> Yes. But not so little anymore.
> I can't believe you remember.

> LUTHER
> I'm surprise you recognize me.

> CONSTANCE
> Oh, how could I forget? All the stories.
> I even remember your dad, Danny—Daniel.
> It's been a million years!?

147

LUTHER
(laughs)
Seems like. Seems like. Your daddy
still with us?

CONSTANCE
No. He passed a few years back.

LUTHER
Oh no. That's too bad.

CONSTANCE
He would've loved this. He would
have loved seeing you.

LUTHER
He was a good boy. He was a good
man. We had us some times.

CONSTANCE
We did. And he loved you so much.
Had a nickname. What was it?
(recalling)
Oh, yes. He called you . . . *Spider*.
Uncle Spider.

Luther laughs. Corina, Buford and Cleo walk over.

LUTHER
I haven't been called that in a
while.

Stan climbs off Tucson's shoulders and walks over to Cleo to
get a better look at Josie.

STAN
(staring at Josie)
Does he bite?

CLEO

Only strangers. The mailman. And
sometimes Bible salesmen.
(looking at Josie)
I wish my great-grand-granny would
have had him. He would've protected
her.

Luther introduces Corina, Buford and Cleo to Constance. Tucson
and Shereyar walk up.

CONSTANCE
(to Luther)
Did you ever think this day would
come?

LUTHER

No, ma'am.
(looking around)
I left a long time ago, and I been gone
ever since.

CONSTANCE

I stayed away, too. But this had to be
done.

LUTHER

Wuddn't nothin' I thought could bring
me back.
(looking around)
But this. I could''ta missed it.

Luther's eyes well up.

LUTHER
(continuing)
My mama died here. We lost
everything. We lost everything we
had. If not for Daniel—if not for

149

LUTHER (CONT'D)
my stepdaddy . . .

A tear runs down Constance's cheek. She wipes it away.

CONSTANCE
We did, too.
(nodding to Tucson)
And his family, as well.

LUTHER
(wiping his eyes)
Ha. Stop that. This is a good day.

Constance smiles. Tucson looks back up at the marker.

TUCSON
This is a great day.

The adults talk.

Members of the crowd take turns taking more pictures in front of
the historical marker.

JUMP CUT:

EXT—FARM ROAD, PRESENT DAY—AFTERNOON
The campfire group is standing in front of and facing the
unveiled historical marker.

CLEVE
It do say our names.

DICK
It say what they done to us.

WILLA
Does it say what they done *with* us?
Where we wuz put low?

150

ALEX
No. No, it don't.
(long pause)
You thank we're piled up in some
pit like Jeff seen?

WILLA
Oh, Lawd. Surely not. Surely.

JEFF
Then, they is lookin' for us? They's
tryin' to find us?

DICK
I have to reckon so. I have to believe
that.

JOHN
(groggily)
Believe what?

SAM
That they wouldn't leave us that way.

CUT TO:

EXT—FARM ROAD, PRESENT DAY—AFTERNOON
CLOSE ON: CLEVE

CAPTION: CLEVELAND LARKIN, 1882-JULY 29, 1910,
INTERRED IN MASS, UNMARKED GRAVE—
WHEREABOUTS UNKNOWN.

CUT TO:

EXT—FARM ROAD, PRESENT DAY—AFTERNOON
CLOSE ON: ALEX

CAPTION: ALEX HOLLEY, 1891-JULY 29, 1910, INTERRED IN MASS, UNMARKED GRAVE—WHEREABOUTS UNKNOWN.

                                    CUT TO:

EXT—FARM ROAD, PRESENT DAY—AFTERNOON
CLOSE ON: JOHN

CAPTION: JOHN HAYS, 1880-JULY 29, 1910, INTERRED IN MASS, UNMARKED GRAVE—WHEREABOUTS UNKNOWN.

                                    CUT TO:

EXT—FARM ROAD, PRESENT DAY—AFTERNOON
CLOSE ON: RAE

CAPTION: RAE THOMPSON, 1894-JULY 29, 1910, INTERRED IN MASS, UNMARKED GRAVE— WHEREABOUTS UNKNOWN.

                                    CUT TO:

EXT—FARM ROAD, PRESENT DAY—AFTERNOON
CLOSE ON: SAM

CAPTION: SAM BAKER, 1892-JULY 29, 1910, INTERRED IN MASS, UNMARKED GRAVE—WHEREABOUTS UNKNOWN.

                                    CUT TO:

EXT—FARM ROAD, PRESENT DAY—AFTERNOON
CLOSE ON: DICK

CAPTION: RICHARD WILSON, 1865-JULY 29, 1910, INTERRED IN MASS, UNMARKED GRAVE— WHEREABOUTS UNKNOWN.

CUT TO:

EXT—FARM ROAD, PRESENT DAY—AFTERNOON
CLOSE ON: JEFF

CAPTION: JEFFREY WILSON, 1882-JULY 29, 1910,
INTERRED IN MASS, UNMARKED GRAVE—
WHEREABOUTS UNKNOWN.

CUT TO:

EXT—FARM ROAD, PRESENT DAY—AFTERNOON
CLOSE ON: WILLA

CAPTION: WILLA CAMPBELL, 1835-JULY 29, 1910,
INTERRED IN MASS, UNMARKED GRAVE—
WHEREABOUTS UNKNOWN.

FADE TO BLACK.

—**BUT WAY BACK** in the black, there is a dim light. It grows
closer and larger and brighter. It's a campfire, and there are
hundreds of black people around it.

BIOS

CONSTANCE HOLLIE-JAWAID

Constance Hollie-Jawaid received a Bachelor's degree in Education and a Master's degree in Counseling and Guidance from Texas A&M-Commerce. She received her Superintendent's Certification from the University of Texas at Arlington and earned a certification in Urban Leadership from Harvard University. Constance began her career in education in 1991 as a middle school English teacher and, since then, she has been a counselor, dean of instruction and a principal. In 2012, she was voted Principal of the Year in Cedar Hill Independent School District. Currently, she serves as a principal for the Dallas Independent School District. She has created programs and delivered workshops at the state and national level related to Culturally Relevant Education, Language Acquisition, Bilingual Education and Working with At-Risk Students. She also serves as the Middle School Ambassador of the National Association of Black School Educators. Currently, she is a Sociology doctoral student at the University of Buea in the west African country of Cameroon. Her dissertation topic is "The Socio-economic Impact of Racial and Ethnic Marginalization."

CHAIS ADRIAN TEAL

At an early age, Chais Adrian Teal began passionately practicing art. He was self-taught and the You-tube era allowed him to develop his craft quickly and study many other artists and mediums. Originally born in Irving, TX, he spent most of his childhood in Bedford, TX, where he became affiliated with the Central Arts nonprofit association. Teal is known for live painting exhibitions with fellow artists Sergio Santos and Juan Zamora at different venues throughout the DFW metroplex.

E. R. BILLS

E. R. Bills is the author of *Texas Obscurities: Stories of the Peculiar, Exceptional and Nefarious* (The History Press, 2013), *The 1910 Slocum Massacre: An Act of Genocide in East Texas* (The History Press, 2014), *Black Holocaust: The Paris Horror and a Legacy of Texas Terror* (Eakin Press, 2015), *Texas Far & Wide: The Tornado With Eyes, Gettysburg's Last Casualty, The Celestial Skipping Stone and Other Tales* (The History Press, 2017), *The San Marcos 10: An Antiwar Protest in Texas* (The History Press, 2019) and Texas Oblivion: Mysterious Disappearances, Escapes and Cover-Ups (The History Press, 2021). He lives in North Texas with his wife, Stacie.

CPSIA information can be obtained
at www.ICGtesting.com
Printed in the USA
LVHW080055260323
742599LV00014B/1309